Additional books by Sandy Saia Lombardo

Rahab, My Story: The Covenant, Two Spies, Jericho, and Salvation

Samuel's Gift for Baby Jesus!

RAHAB

My Story

—— DISCUSSION GUIDE ——

A JOURNEY FROM SINFULNESS TO FAITHFULNESS

SANDY SAIA LOMBARDO

WESTBOW
PRESS®
A DIVISION OF THOMAS NELSON
& ZONDERVAN

WestBow Press books may be ordered through booksellers or by contacting:

WestBow Press
A Division of Thomas Nelson & Zondervan
1663 Liberty Drive
Bloomington, IN 47403
www.westbowpress.com
1 (866) 928-1240

Because of the dynamic nature of the Internet, any web addresses or links contained in this book may have changed since publication and may no longer be valid. The views expressed in this work are solely those of the author and do not necessarily reflect the views of the publisher, and the publisher hereby disclaims any responsibility for them.

Scripture quotations are from The Holy Bible, English Standard Version® (ESV®), copyright © 2001 by Crossway, a publishing ministry of Good News Publishers. Used by permission. All rights reserved.

Cover image credit: Jonathan Winchell (www.winchellarts.com)
Interior drawings by Nicole Saia

This is a work of fiction. All of the characters, names, incidents, organizations, and dialogue in this novel are either the products of the author's imagination or are used fictitiously.

Any people depicted in stock imagery provided by Thinkstock are models, and such images are being used for illustrative purposes only.
Certain stock imagery © Thinkstock.

ISBN: 978-1-5127-4100-1 (sc)
ISBN: 978-1-5127-4101-8 (e)

Library of Congress Control Number: 2016907444

Print information available on the last page.

WestBow Press rev. date: 06/30/2016

To my husband, Tom (Lumpy!):

Thank you for listening to me go on and on about Rahab and for always encouraging me as I prayed to confirm that the Lord wanted me to write this discussion guide. Thank you for allowing me the many hours needed to sort through all of my notes, to check and recheck Scriptures, and to continually pray for wisdom and guidance.

Many times our *together* time turned into my *project* time, but that was fine with you. You have given me ample space to pray and ask the Lord to guide my thoughts and to make this guide something that would answer questions about the love of God, about our sinful state, and about how we can journey from sinfulness to faithfulness.

Love you "Always and Forever" (the song you sang to me at our wedding).

To my children, Tommi and Tony:

I *so* love you both. I am thankful beyond measure for having you in my life, for my grandchildren, and for the way we have grown together in the Lord. You have taught me so much.

To my dear friends Richard and Denise:

Thank you for your confirmation of this discussion guide and for the great suggestions. God used you to abundantly bless me.

To my dear friend Cheryl:

Thank you for patiently editing my many mistakes. I hope I have learned at least a little of what you have attempted to teach me.

To my dear niece, Nicole:

Thank you for using your artistic talent to create a page at the end of each discussion day; giving us time to pause, meditate on the Lord, and color a beautiful picture based on Scripture.

As anyone can see, it does take a village!

My prayer is that this discussion guide will plant the seeds of faith, water the buds of growing desires to know the Lord, build a strong foundation to grow on, and point to the One who loves us, desires a relationship with us, and wants to abundantly bless us!

Come to me, all who labor and are heavy laden, and I will give you rest.

— Matthew 11:28

CONTENTS

INTRODUCTION

P raise God! You have joined me for this book discussion about the life of Rahab of Jericho: Rahab, the prostitute; Rahab, the forgiven; Rahab, the faithful. If you have not read the book, *Rahab, My Story: The Covenant, Two Spies, Jericho, and Salvation*[1] yet, you will still be blessed by this discussion guide, for we will be quoting quite a bit from the book, and we will be immersed in the Bible, learning the very character of the one and only, true God of heaven and earth.

Rahab, My Story is a historical fiction book on the life of Rahab in the Old Testament of the Bible. We will peek into Rahab's life and try to understand the transformation she likely went through when she heard about and prayed to know the only true God, Yahweh. Not a great deal is written about Rahab, but what we discover between the lines of what *was* written is powerful, life-altering, and noteworthy. In fact, in the book of Hebrews in the New Testament, Rahab is acknowledged for her great faith. Now that is quite a transformation.

As I shared in my book, *Rahab, My Story*, I spent many nights dreaming of Rahab and later wondered what those dreams meant. After much prayer, I believed that God would have me share with you the many trials and much rejoicing that Rahab possibly experienced in her journey from sinfulness to faithfulness. I will share with you several similarities I had with Rahab's journey. Could it be that your life parallels Rahab's life too? Have you journeyed from sinfulness to faithfulness? Could that be your heart's desire?

Since you have joined me, I assume that we have something in common. You probably have thought about God. You may be seeking answers, or you may be just considering

---

[1] Sandy Saia Lombardo, *Rahab, My Story: The Covenant, Two Spies, Jericho, and Salvation* (WestBow Press Publishing, 2015).

whether or not you *do* want to believe and learn anything at all about God. Are you questioning the truth of the many things you have heard others say about God's loving His people and bringing peace and joy into their lives, or about His unimaginable promises of help, love, guidance, forgiveness, wisdom, hope, and an intimate relationship with Him?

This discussion guide will be a great place to begin looking for answers, a great place for a new beginning.

Maybe you believe with all of your heart, soul, mind, and strength that God *is* the creator of all things, and you desire to follow and obey only Him. Okay. We will be reaffirming what we already believe and maybe even increasing our love for the Lord by being in the Word and reading what our heavenly Father has to say to us.

This discussion guide will possibly help us to increase our faith and renew our commitment to believe, trust, and obey God.

Let us learn together, ask questions, search for answers, pray for wisdom, and be blessed.

I hope you enjoy your pause at the end of each discussion day. Treat yourself to a time of meditation, while coloring a beautiful picture as you reflect on God's blessings in our lives.

"You will know the truth, and the truth will set you free" (John 8:32).

WHO IS YAHWEH? WHAT WAS RAHAB'S PROFESSION?

The subtitle of the book *Rahab, My Story* is *The Covenant, Two Spies, Jericho, and Salvation*. For this discussion guide, I think we will consider the subtitle to be *Forgiven, Grafted In, Faithful, and Blessed*. After all, that is what is so monumental in the story of Rahab.

If you read the book *Rahab, My Story*, you saw that Rahab's life was completely transformed when she called out to Yahweh, the only true God of heaven and earth, to be her God.

Who Is Yahweh (God)?

A spiritual and saving knowledge of God is the greatest need of every human creature.[1]

"Great is our Lord, and abundant in power; his understanding is beyond measure" (Psalm 147:5).

In the first and second chapters of Genesis, we are told that God is the Creator of the heavens and the earth, the day and the night, the waters, and all the vegetation. In Genesis 1:20, God said, "Let the waters swarm with swarms of living creatures, and let birds fly

---

[1] Arthur W. Pink. *The Attributes of God*. Baker Books of Baker Book House Company, 1975.

above the earth across the expanse of the heavens." Next, livestock, creeping things, and the beasts of the earth were created. God then created man in His own image, breathing life into man's nostrils. From one of man's ribs, God created woman and gave the couple dominion over everything that moved on earth. God saw all that He had made and said that it was very good (Genesis 1:31).

"When I look at your heavens, the work of your fingers, the moon and the stars, which you have set in place, what is man that you are mindful of him, and the son of man that you care for him?" (Psalm 8:3–4).

"He determines the number of the stars; he gives to all of them their names" (Psalm 147:4).

"Let them praise the name of the LORD! For he commanded and they were created" (Psalm 148:5).

"For by him all things were created, in heaven and on earth, visible and invisible, whether thrones or dominions or rulers or authorities—all things were created through him and for him" (Colossians 1:16).

"Do you not fear me? declares the LORD. Do you not tremble before me? I placed the sand as the boundary for the sea, a perpetual barrier that it cannot pass; though the waves toss, they cannot prevail; though they roar, they cannot pass over it" (Jeremiah 5:22).

"Worthy are you, our Lord and God, to receive glory and honor and power, for you created all things, and by your will they existed and were created" (Revelation 4:11).

God is the creator of all things. God set the stars in their places and has named each and every one of them. Creation was a plan, a glorious and perfect plan. Are you beginning to get just a glimpse of how magnificent God is?

I know what you are thinking: how did He do it? I don't know how God created everything. Isaiah 55:9 tells us, "For as the heavens are higher than the earth, so are my ways higher than your ways and my thoughts than your thoughts." I accept that explanation. In our study, we will learn and understand more about God through what is revealed about Him in Scripture.

What Is the Trinity?

Trinity is the union of three persons (Father, Son, and Holy Spirit) in one Godhead, or the threefold personality of the one Divine Being.[2]

You will not find the word *trinity* in the Bible, but you will read about the Trinity in many Scriptures.

I believe we will go to Isaiah 55:9 again when attempting to understand the Trinity, and then we can search the Scriptures for revelation. Below are a few Scriptures that point to the Trinity.

"Go therefore and make disciples of all nations, baptizing them in the name of the Father and of the Son and of the Holy Spirit" (Matthew 28:19).

"Then God said, 'Let us make man in our image, after our likeness'" (Genesis 1:26).

Jesus said, "But when the Helper comes, whom I will send to you from the Father, the Spirit of truth, who proceeds from the Father, he will bear witness about me" (John 15:26).

God reveals Himself to us through Scripture. He desires that we come to know, trust, and obey Him. We can better understand God through reading His Word, meditating on it, and praying for wisdom. Through this discussion guide, let us do just that—pray for wisdom in understanding what we discover in each discussion day.

God is referred to by different names relating to His character or attributes. You may have heard the names *El Shaddai* (Lord God Almighty), *Adonai* (Lord or Master), and *Yahweh* (Lord, or Jehovah). God is also referred to as Savior, Redeemer, Messiah, Lord, Master, Holy One, Judge, Teacher, Creator, Shepherd, King of Kings, Lord of Lords, Lamb of God, King of Glory, Author, Comforter, Abba Father, Prince of Peace, I AM, Everlasting Father, Wonderful Counselor, Bread of Life, and many other names. As you speak each name, do you get a picture in your mind of the wondrous greatness of God, which is beyond understanding?

---

[2] *Dictionary.com.*

"Let them praise the name of the Lord, for his name alone is exalted; his majesty is above earth and heaven" (Psalm 148:13).

We read about another wonderful name of God in the following Scripture: "Behold, the virgin shall conceive and bear a son, and they shall call his name Immanuel [God with us]" (Matthew 1:23).

Are you seeing more and more clearly the *immense* magnitude of God? We will look at several attributes of God in the discussion days that follow.

In chapters one and two of *Rahab, My Story*, we learn who Rahab is and about her life.

In the heart of Jericho, Rahab had a lucrative business as an innkeeper. Travelers—and the local men—loved to lodge at Rahab's inn, because she provided them with much more than the basic necessities. Being able to afford the best of everything wasn't enough for Rahab. Something was missing. From the many patrons who lodged at Rahab's inn, she heard stories about the Israelite people and their God, Yahweh. She heard about Yahweh's love for His chosen people, about the Promised Land that He would give to His people one day, and about a covenant made many years earlier between Yahweh and a faithful follower, Abraham. Rahab eventually made the decision to pray to this God and ask for His help.

You can read about Rahab in chapters 2 and 6 in the book of Joshua.

Rahab also told us how content she was with her life. She described all of her material possessions: the best wines, linens, and jewelry. And she told us how all the women of Jericho envied the clothes she wore. All of her material possessions were very important to Rahab.

Let's list some things we consider to be very important in our lives, things we give most of our attention to.

_____   _____

_____   _____

_____   _____

_____   _____

_____   _____

Now, let's see how God's Word, the Bible, tells us to view these important things.

"But seek _____ the _____ _____ _____ and _____
_____, and all these things will be added to you" (Matthew 6:33).

"You shall have _____ other _____ before me" (Exodus 20:3).

"You shall _____the Lord your _____ with all your _____ and
with all your _____ and with all your _____ and with all your
_____, and your _____ as _____ "
(Luke 10:27).

"God _____ down from heaven on the children of man to see if there are any who
_____ who _____ _____ _____ " (Psalm 53:2).

"There is a way that seems _____ to a man, but its end is the way to _____ "
(Proverbs 14:12).

If we are consumed with gaining material things, striving to make it up the ladder of success, belonging to all sorts of organizations, being too busy with our husbands' or children's lives, traveling the world, gaining more and more knowledge, or maybe even volunteering too much, have we made something else number one in our lives? None of the above is wrong, as long as we keep God first!

How did you do with having things in the right priority? I fail occasionally. Okay, I fail often. I frequently allow different things to consume my life, pushing God to the sidelines. I try to take control of things, but that, of course, is what God wants to do.

As I read devotional books, I get the picture that God wants us to trust in Him completely rather than to rely on ourselves. He wants us to seek Him first, and as we read in Matthew 6:33, all other things will be added to us. So let us not strive to have everything orderly in our lives all of the time, which, as we have all probably experienced, is impossible. I realize that I waste much of my time and energy attempting to live a very organized, structured life.

I am a bit OCD (obsessive-compulsive disorder) in all that I do, so naturally I strive to have that organized, structured life. I believe I fall into the *counters and arrangers* part of OCD, which means I am obsessed with order and symmetry.

Being a dental technician in the United States Navy for almost eleven years (active duty and reserves) fed right into my OCD. I was "sharp wave" of my company in boot camp. I had the most perfectly made bed, the shiniest spit-shined shoes, and the most crisply ironed uniforms in my unit. In the navy, you would say that I was "squared away."

These days, I would have to admit that I still love how perfectly I fold towels, make beds, dust higher than I can see (because most of my friends are taller than I am), vacuum with a beautiful pattern on a rug, keep neat records, evenly space the hangers in my closet, iron creases in clothes, etc. You know what I mean? I am a nut! I drive myself crazy trying to maintain a tidy and structured life. I searched the Scriptures to determine if there was another way—a better choice that I could make rather than depending on just my own efforts. The following Scriptures helped me:

"If they listen and serve him [God], they complete their days in prosperity, and their years in pleasantness" (Job 36:11).

"Serve the LORD with gladness! Come into his presence with singing!" (Psalm 100:2).

"I sought the LORD, and he answered me and delivered me from all my fears. Those who look to him are radiant, and their faces shall never be ashamed. This poor man cried, and the LORD heard him and saved him out of all his troubles. The angel of the LORD encamps around those who fear him, and delivers them. Oh, taste and see that the LORD is good! Blessed is the man who takes refuge in him!" (Psalm 34:4–8).

I found instruction in the Bible on how to live, and then I had a choice to make: drive myself crazy striving for perfection, or, as the saying goes, "Let go and let God." We all must make a decision to allow God to have control of our lives, or we can choose to keep the control ourselves and stumble through life continually in search of our purpose. What will you choose?

Scriptures to Consider

"The LORD is on my side; I will not _____. What can man do to me?" (Psalm 118:6).

"_____ not, for I am with you" (Isaiah 43:5a).

"But let _____who take refuge in_____ rejoice; let them ever sing for_____, and spread your _____ over them, that those who _____ your name may _____in you" (Psalm 5:11).

"Now to him who is able to keep you from _____ and to _____ you _____before the presence of his _____ with great joy, to the only God our Savior, through Jesus Christ our Lord, be glory, majesty, dominion, and authority, through _____ _____ our Lord, before all time and now and forever. Amen" (Jude vv. 24–25).

"____ _____ shall be able to stand before _____ all the days of your life. Just as I was with Moses, so I will be with you. I will not _____ _____ _____ _____ _____" (Joshua 1:5).

"The thief comes only to steal and kill and destroy. ____ came that they may have _____ and have it _____" (John 10:10).

As you read those Scriptures, did you let them sink into your heart? If we take refuge in God we will be glad, filled with joy, and rejoice. We will be as faultless before God, and He promises to never leave or forsake us. What comfort we can find in those promises!

Oh, to have someone who loves us unconditionally, who is in our corner, on our side, cheering us on, always with us, providing for our needs; someone who will pick us up when we fall, who will forgive us, who will listen to our hearts, who will hold us when we are sad, who will rejoice when we rejoice, who will answer our prayers, who will lead us down a path of righteousness, who has prepared a place for us, and who will be waiting for us at the finish line to take us home!

No more long faces for those of us who love the Lord! Agreed?

How did God speak to you through our Scriptures this discussion day?

_____

_____

_____

_____

"The Lord be with your spirit. Grace be with you" (2 Timothy 4:22).

I AM........ Love

AUTHOR OF LIFE

LOVE
Redeemer Savior HOLY ONE

Deliverer GOD Creator

KING Love Holy Ghost Shepherd

JESUS Lamb Messiah

LOVE Bread of Life

Ever-last-ing Christ Adonai LOVE

Judge LOVE JEHOVAH

Counselor El Shaddai

Lord Father Yahweh

Teacher Abba Master

THE COVENANT AND PROMISED LAND: WE ALL MISS THE MARK

Did what we read in "Discussion Day One" make sense to you? I thought it gave us a lot to consider. Are we content with our lives just the way they are? Do we really know our purpose in life? Have we set the right goals for our lives, if we have set any at all? Is our focus in the right place? Or do you feel like Rahab felt: life is going along okay, you have material wealth and you are doing just fine with your own plan for your life?

Let's dig into "Discussion Day Two" and discover more treasures. Let's continue to unwrap the gift that is ours—if we accept it. We'll talk a lot more about that gift in the following discussion days.

I believe we all want to be happy in life, but are we searching in the right places for happiness? What do you recall when you think of happy times? Going on a date with someone special? Buying a new car, new shoes, or a new dress? How about a new apartment or home? Are you someone who is always planning the next vacation or the next exciting party? Would you say that, just maybe, your happiness depends on all of these things, these happenings?

Let's consider how we feel when we are unable to plan more fun parties or shop until we drop. What happens when someone we love dies or if we lose our job or home? How do we handle those disappointments? Do we have some special joy in our lives that will carry us through difficult times? Is there a deep, meaningful joy that will comfort us when disappointment or depression tries to envelop us, send us over the edge, or overwhelm us beyond what we think we can handle? As we continue on in our discussion guide, I hope that you will come to know and believe that putting our complete trust in Jesus is what will give us that joy we are looking for. Trusting in our Lord Jesus is what will carry us through any and all circumstances.

Let's read the following Scriptures and write the word *joy* in every blank.

"You make known to me the path of life; in your presence there is fullness of _____; at your right hand are pleasures forevermore" (Psalm 16:11).

> Is fullness of joy—Not partial joy; not imperfect joy; not joy intermingled with pain and sorrow; not joy which, though in itself real, does not satisfy the desires of the soul, as is the case with much of the happiness which we experience in this life—but joy, full, satisfying, unalloyed, unclouded, unmingled with anything that would diminish its fullness or its brightness; joy that will not be diminished, as all earthly joys must be, by the feeling that it must soon come to an end.[1]

It is difficult to imagine that kind of complete, uninterrupted joy that comes from our Lord. The definition of joy we just read will help us to better understand what fullness of joy means in the following Scriptures.

"For you have been my help, and in the shadow of your wings I will sing for _____" (Psalm 63:7).

"My lips will shout for _____, when I sing praises to you; my soul also, which you have redeemed" (Psalm 71:23).

"The meadows clothe themselves with flocks, the valleys deck themselves with grain, they shout and sing together for _____" (Psalm 65:13).

"Let the rivers clap their hands; let the hills sing for _____ together" (Psalm 98:8).

---

[1] Albert Barnes, *Barnes' Notes on the Bible* (1798–1870).

"After listening to the king, they went on their way. And behold, the star that they had seen when it rose went before them until it came to rest over the place where the child was. When they saw the star, they rejoiced exceedingly with great_____" (Matthew 2:9–10).

"And the angel said to them, 'Fear not, for behold, I bring you good news of great _____ that will be for all the people'" (Luke 2:10).

Do you know what that "good news of great joy for all the people" was—and is? We will be discussing just that in the following discussion days.

I recently purchased an engraved piece of wood that reads,

> **"Forever, For Always, and No Matter What!"**

This is how God loves us, friend.

"There is therefore now no condemnation for those who are in Christ Jesus" (Romans 8:1).

In chapters one and two of *Rahab, My Story*, Rahab said she was content with her life, yet she began having questions about Yahweh, the God of the Israelites, when she heard how He loved and cared for His people. From travelers who lodged at her inn, Rahab heard talk about a *covenant* made between Yahweh and one of His chosen people, Abraham.

Why were there chosen people? She wondered. She also heard about a promised land. What was a promised land? She heard how Yahweh had parted the Red Sea so His people could safely pass through when they were exiting captivity in Egypt, and how He had sweetened bitter water in the desert so His people would not thirst. Who could do such things? Rahab began questioning her beliefs and lifestyle, and she desired to know more about the God of the Israelite people.

> A *covenant* is a sacred agreement between God and a person or group of people. God sets specific conditions and promises to bless us as we obey.[2]

---

[2] *Wikipedia Free Encyclopedia*

> *Promised Land*: In Genesis 12:1–3, God made a covenant with Abraham about a particular land that His chosen people would possess one day.

"Now the LORD said to Abram, 'Go from your country and your kindred and your father's house to the land that I will show you [Promised Land]. And I will make of you a great nation, and I will bless you and make your name great, so that you will be a blessing. I will bless those who bless you, and him who dishonors you I will curse, and in you all the families of the earth shall be blessed'" (Genesis 12:1–3).

Those very blessings that God said would flow through Abram (his name was changed to Abraham by God in Genesis 17:5) to the rest of the world are blessings that you and I can receive. We can be God's chosen people too. Praise God!

God's people throughout all time have been recipients of blessings through Abraham if they have been counted as faithful, as Abraham was. As a new believer in Yahweh, Rahab began to understand that those blessings she heard about could be hers also if she turned from her sinful life and followed Yahweh.

"We say that faith was counted to Abraham as righteousness" (Romans 4:9b).

In chapter two of *Rahab, My Story*, Rahab told us how she stood by the city gates listening to travelers tell stories about Yahweh and His followers. She wondered if Yahweh could love someone like her. She began thinking that just maybe there was more to life. Maybe all of her possessions did not make her happy and complete. Maybe Rahab was not content with her life after all.

Do you sometimes wonder why you were even born? *Is there more to life? Is there some purpose for my life?* I have had those thoughts. Does the Bible give us answers to these questions? Yes!

The book of Ephesians answers some of our questions.

> "Blessed be the God and Father of our Lord Jesus Christ, who has blessed us in Christ with every spiritual blessing in the heavenly places, even as he chose us in him before the foundation of the world, that we should be holy

and blameless before him. In love he predestined us for adoption as sons through Jesus Christ, according to the purpose of his will, to the praise of his glorious grace, with which he has blessed us in the Beloved. In him we have redemption through his blood, the forgiveness of our trespasses, according to the riches of his grace, which he lavished upon us, in all wisdom and insight making known to us the mystery of his will, according to his purpose, which he set forth in Christ as a plan for the fullness of time, to unite all things in him, things in heaven and things on earth. In him we have obtained an inheritance, having been predestined according to the purpose of him who works all things according to the counsel of his will, so that we who were the first to hope in Christ might be to the praise of his glory. In him you also, when you heard the word of truth, the gospel of your salvation, and believed in him, were sealed with the promised Holy Spirit, who is the guarantee of our inheritance until we acquire possession of it, to the praise of his glory." (Ephesians 1:3–14)

What a lot to take in! I really think we would need many weeks to study all of the glorious truths in those Scriptures. For now, can we just agree to look at the big picture? Our following discussion days will help us to see and understand those Scriptures more clearly. Let us look at what the apostle Paul said when writing to the people in Ephesus, which follows the passage we just read.

"I do not cease to give thanks for you, remembering you in my prayers, that the God of our Lord Jesus Christ, the Father of glory, may give you a spirit of wisdom and of revelation in the knowledge of him, having the eyes of your hearts enlightened, that you may know what is the hope to which he has called you, what are the riches of his glorious inheritance in the saints, and what is the immeasurable greatness of his power toward us who believe, according to the working of his great might that he worked in Christ when he raised him from the dead and seated him at his right hand in the heavenly places, far above all rule and authority and power and dominion, and above every name that is named, not only in this age but also in the one to come. And he put all things under his feet and gave him as head over all things to the church, which is his body, the fullness of him who fills all in all." (Ephesians 1:16–23)

I agree with you that this is a lot to grasp, but this is the basis of what we will be discovering as we continue through our discussion guide. Let us be patient and pray for wisdom as we continue on.

Psalm 139:16 tells us that God's eyes saw our unformed substance. In His book were written the days that were formed for us—every one of them—when as yet there were none of them.

God loves us! We were made for God's pleasure. Think about that for a minute. The one and only Supreme Being, the creator of all things, created us to be the focus of His love. He loves us and wants a relationship with us. Can you really imagine that? We are blessed.

Rahab realized that she had been living a terribly sinful life, and she questioned whether Yahweh could care about someone like her. After all, she had lived only to please herself, not caring about anyone else (*Rahab, My Story*, 13.)

Maybe you believe that God loves only *good* people. You know the ones I am talking about: the ones who are pictured on the covers of magazines and nominated for very special, prestigious awards.

Look at all of the amazing people in the world, I used to think. *People who feed the hungry, people who build homes for the homeless, people who stand for worthy causes, people who save lives, people who fight to keep our country free, and people who share the love of the true God all around the world with those who worship pagan gods.*

Oh, how small I felt! I could not measure up to all of the heroes in the world. So, my thinking was that God loves those worthy people, not useless, insignificant people like me. Have you ever felt that way?

Let's look as some Scriptures that will help us to understand how God views us.

Scriptures to Consider

"As it is written; _____ is righteous, no, not one; _____ _____ understands; _____ _____ seeks for God. _____ have turned aside; together they have become worthless; _____ _____ does good, _____ _____ _____" (Romans 3:10–12).

"For _____ have _____ and fall short of the glory of God" (Romans 3:23).

"For the wages of sin is _____, but the free gift of God is _____ _____ in Christ _____ our Lord" (Romans 6:23).

"_____, and it will be given to you; _____, and you will find; _____, and it will be opened to you. For everyone who asks _____, and the one who seeks _____, and to the one who knocks it will be _____" (Matthew 7:7–8).

"For God _____ _____ the _____, that he _____ his only _____, that whoever _____ in _____ should not _____ but have_____ _____" (John 3:16).

God *so* loved the world, the Scripture says. God *so* loves us, not *just* loves us. If we have been blessed with children, grandchildren, or someone very special in our lives, how do we say we love them? To emphasize how much we love them, might we say, "I *so* love my child or grandchild," or "I love them *so* much"? God is attempting to have us understand *how much* He loves us, not that He just loves us.

"For while we were still weak, at the right time Christ died for the ungodly. For one will scarcely die for a righteous person—though perhaps for a good person one would dare even to die—but God shows his love for us in that while we were still sinners, Christ died for us" (Romans 5:6–8).

"For if while we were enemies we were reconciled to God by the death of his Son, much more, now that we are reconciled, shall we be saved by his life" (Romans 5:10).

Is it beginning to sound like God loves sinners, not only people who (we think) do good things? Read Romans 3:23 again. For *all* have sinned. *All* fall short. That includes you, me, and *all* of the good people we know. How can that be? You ask. Let's keep searching for answers.

When you think about the word *sin*, what comes to mind? Do you automatically feel badly? Guilty? The word *sin* makes me feel like I did something I shouldn't have, according to God's laws. The word *sin* also makes me think about the times when I knew I *should have* done something but neglected to do it.

It may also be helpful when describing sin to mention that the word is an archery term that means "missing the mark." God's standard is perfection, and anything short of that is sin.

So, is Scripture saying that *no one* is righteous? *No one* seeks God? *All* have turned away? *No one* does good, *no not one*? Are we included in that group of "no ones"? Yes! We are all sinners. We *all* fall short of the glory of God. We *all* miss the mark (perfection). We *all* sin. We have a lot to think about, don't we? Let's keep searching.

How did God speak to you through our Scriptures this discussion day?

_____

_____

_____

_____

"Now to him who is able to do far more abundantly than all that we ask or think, according to the power at work within us, to him be glory in the church and in Christ Jesus throughout all generations, forever and ever. Amen" (Ephesians 3:20–21).

SALVATION, GRACE, MERCY, AND TRUST

"Discussion Day Two" gave us a lot to think about. Did you like our little talk about happiness? It sounded so good in the beginning, but then we had to consider what would happen when all of the exciting and fun things in life cease to exist. Really, what then?

Should we evaluate our lives and assess our goals? In what direction is our life heading? Where will we end up? When we die, are things just over? Does anything we've done in life really matter? These are a few deep, eternal questions that deserve serious consideration.

We are given such great hope in knowing that when everything in our lives seems to be falling apart—when we lose our job, when a family member or a friend dies, when we can't pay our bills, when we are hungry, when we suffer with some terminal illness, when we lose our home, when we have trials upon trials, when we have unresolved conflict with someone, and when nothing at all seems to be going right—we are not to give up or give in.

"Count it all joy, my brothers, when you meet trials of various kinds, for you know that the testing of your faith produces steadfastness. And let steadfastness have its full effect, that you may be perfect and complete, lacking in nothing" (James 1:2–4).

There is joy for those of us who put our trust in God. Do you remember reading in "Discussion Day One" that our Lord will never leave us or forsake us? Claim that promise. Find rest, joy, and peace in Him.

God says we are His children. He lavishes His love on us. "See what kind of love the Father has given to us, that we should be called children of God" (1 John 3:1a).

"For you, O Lord, are good and forgiving, abounding in steadfast love to all who call upon you" (Psalm 86:5).

"But you, O Lord, are a God merciful and gracious, slow to anger and abounding in steadfast love and faithfulness" (Psalm 86:15).

What did Rahab do when she realized that her plan for her life wasn't working out too well?

In chapter three of *Rahab, My Story*, Rahab evaluated her life and determined that she had been heading down a path of disobedience and destruction for some time. After hearing many accounts of Yahweh's love and concern for His people, she made the decision to call out to Him and plead for His help. She had been convicted of her sinful life and desperately desired to change.

Rahab wanted to know Yahweh and to trust and follow Him alone. She prayed that God would forgive her, save her, and call her one of His very own.

What does *save* or *salvation* mean? Who can be saved?

Salvation is available to all of us—no matter what we look like, how young or old we are, or how sinful we have been. The Bible tells us in Romans 10:9 that if you confess with your mouth that Jesus is Lord and believe in your heart that God raised him from the dead, you will be saved. Only because of what Jesus did for us on the cross can we stand justified (not guilty) before our holy God. We will be searching Scriptures for further explanations.

Many Scriptures in the Old Testament spoke of the One to come who would save mankind from his sins. Below, read one Scripture from Isaiah in the Old Testament. Additional Scriptures from the New Testament follow.

"For to us a child is born, to us a son is given; and the government shall be upon his shoulder, and His name shall be called Wonderful Counselor, Mighty God, Everlasting Father, Prince of Peace" (Isaiah 9:6).

> In the sixth month the angel Gabriel was sent from God to a city of Galilee named Nazareth, to a virgin betrothed to a man whose name was Joseph, of the house of David. And the virgin's name was Mary. And he came to her and said, "Greetings, O favored one, the Lord is with you!" But she was greatly troubled at the saying, and tried to discern what sort of greeting this might be. And the angel said to her, "Do not be afraid, Mary, for you have found favor with God. And behold, you will conceive in your womb and bear a son, and you shall call his name Jesus. He will be great and will be called the Son of the Most High. And the Lord God will give to him the throne of his father David, and he will reign over the house of Jacob forever, and of his kingdom there will be no end. (Luke 1:26–33)

"For Christ also suffered once for sins, the righteous for the unrighteous, that he might bring us to God, being put to death in the flesh but made alive in the spirit" (1 Peter 3:18).

"For the grace of God has appeared, bringing salvation for all people, training us to renounce ungodliness and worldly passions, and to live self-controlled, upright, and godly lives in the present age, waiting for our blessed hope, the appearing of the glory of our great God and Savior Jesus Christ, who gave himself for us to redeem us from all lawlessness and to purify for himself a people for his own possession who are zealous for good works" (Titus 2:11–14).

God had a plan—a perfect plan.

In chapter three of *Rahab, My Story*, Rahab told us that it was difficult leaving her old sinful habits behind, but her heart, her life, and her desires were changing, and she was thankful. She said that fellowship with other believers helped her, and she questioned how God and others could love her—having knowledge of her former life.

Rahab was amazed at the many stories told about Abraham's faith, especially when he obediently left his home and everything he knew to travel to an unknown land (Genesis

12), and when he believed God when he was told that he would have a son by his wife, Sarah, who was many years past child-bearing age (Genesis 15).

The apostle Paul talked about his own struggle with sin in the book of Romans.

> For we know that the law is spiritual, but I am of the flesh, sold under sin. For I do not understand my own actions. For I do not do what I want, but I do the very thing I hate. Now if I do what I do not want, I agree with the law, that it is good. So now it is no longer I who do it, but sin that dwells within me. For I know that nothing good dwells in me, that is, in my flesh. For I have the desire to do what is right, but not the ability to carry it out. For I do not do the good I want, but the evil I do not want is what I keep on doing. Now if I do what I do not want, it is no longer I who do it, but sin that dwells within me. (Romans 7:14–20)

Sound familiar? Do we struggle with sin in our own lives? Sin is anything we put before God—an addiction, envy, idolatry, gossip, pride, sexual immorality, etc. We can add to that list anything that we personally struggle with, not to condemn ourselves, but to be made aware of our shortcomings.

What about *temptation*?

The word *temptation* conjures up many thoughts. At times we may feel tempted to do or say something that we know is wrong. We just *know* it is wrong, but the desire to act on the thoughts is so difficult to resist! Do you agree? What can we do? Let us understand that Satan uses temptation or difficult situations to try to lead us astray from God. Scripture tells us that God uses trials or difficult situations to grow us and lead us to Him.

"More than that, we rejoice in our sufferings, knowing that suffering produces endurance, and endurance produces character, and character produces hope" (Romans 5:3–4).

Satan, the deceiver, would love to see us fall into sin. He would love for us not to seek after God. It is very important that we know and recognize who Satan is and what his intentions are.

Satan means "adversary, accuser." When used as a proper name, the Hebrew word so rendered has the article: "*the* adversary." In the New Testament it is used interchangeably with *Diabolos*, or the Devil, and is so used more than thirty times. He is also called the dragon, the old serpent, the prince of this world, the prince of the power of the air, the god of this world, and the spirit that now worketh in the children of disobedience. The distinct personality of Satan and his activity among men are thus obviously recognized. He tempted our Lord in the wilderness. He is "Beelzebub," the prince of the devils. He is the constant enemy of God, of Christ, of the divine kingdom, of the followers of Christ, and of all truth. He is full of falsehood and all malice, exciting and seducing mankind to evil in every possible way. His power is very great in the world. He is a "roaring lion, seeking whom he may devour." Men are said to be "taken captive by him." Christians are warned against his "devices" and are called on to "resist" him. Christ redeems His people from "him that had the power of death, that is, the devil." Satan has the "power of death," not as lord, but simply as executioner.[1]

"In their case the god of this world has blinded the minds of the unbelievers, to keep them from seeing the light of the gospel of the glory of Christ, who is the image of God" (2 Corinthians 4:4).

"For we do not wrestle against flesh and blood, but against the rulers, against the authorities, against the cosmic powers over this present darkness, against the spiritual forces of evil in the heavenly places" (Ephesians 6:12).

"You are of your father the devil, and your will is to do your father's desires. He was a murderer from the beginning, and has nothing to do with the truth, because there is no truth in him. When he lies, he speaks out of his own character, for he is a liar and the father of lies" (John 8:44).

Do you understand that Satan is pure evil? That definition from *Easton's Bible Dictionary* warned us that Satan is like a roaring lion, seeking whom he may devour. As Christians, we are warned to resist him. We need to be aware of the forces fighting for us—or against us. Be strong in the Lord, friends. Know Him, stay close to Him, and be safe in Him.

---

[1] M. G. Easton, MA, DD, *Illustrated Bible Dictionary*, 1897.

"But let all who take refuge in you rejoice; let them ever sing for joy, and spread your protection over them, that those who love your name may exult in you. For you bless the righteous, O LORD; you cover him with favor as with a shield" (Psalm 5:11–12).

"Be glad in the LORD, and rejoice, O righteous, and shout for joy, all you upright in heart!" (Psalm 32:11).

I feel like we should take a minute to pray.

Dear Lord, please protect us all from the one who wants to bring chaos into our lives; make us worried, fearful, and anxious; make us have wrong motives; and keep us from knowing and following our Creator and Savior. Please write your Word on our hearts and keep us from falling into temptation. You promised to never leave us nor forsake us. We claim that promise! We love you, and we pray this in the magnificent name of our Lord and Savior, Jesus.

"Make your face shine upon your servant, and teach me your statutes" (Psalm 119:135).

Are there bad habits in our lives that we would love to change? Do we sometimes feel like it is just impossible to change old habits? Can we feel like complete failures at times? Is our struggle so difficult that it seems easier to just give up on trying to change? Have you had those thoughts?

Many churches offer a great program for people struggling with many kinds of addictions. Celebrate Recovery (*celebraterecovery.com*) may be the bridge you need to conquer the addictions that trap you, preventing you from crossing over to recovery.

Think about some things in your life that you may want to change. Write them down as a reminder to pray for God's help. Let's desire to change anything that would be more important to us than God.

_____

_____

_____

_____

Scriptures to Consider

"When I am _____, I put my _____ in _____" (Psalm 56:3).

"_____ in the _____ with _____ your _____, and do _____ lean on your _____ understanding. In _____ your ways _____ him, and _____ will make your straight your _____" (Proverbs 3:5–6).

"My _____ is _____ for you, for my _____ is made _____ in _____" (2 Corinthians 12:9).

When we learn to completely trust God—not ourselves—for all things, oh what peace we will have in knowing that He is, indeed, in control of our lives!

A friend gave me a poem, years ago when I was going through a trial I could not see an end to. It spoke about the fact that any trial we are dealing with has likely gone by God and Christ before it has reached us. It went on to say that if some trial has come into our lives, we must not become overwhelmed but must understand that there may be a great lesson to learn through the trial, one that we may eventually see as a blessing. We must attempt not to become overly worried but to have the peace of God in our lives through the trial.

I can be a slow learner at times, but when I began to trust God completely and know that I was His, I was assured that my heavenly Father knew what was best for me. He knew where I needed to grow spiritually, and He worked—and continues to work—in my life to make me more like Him. He is perfecting me through all circumstances, some of which are great victories, and some of which are complete failures. We are refined as we endure all types of trials and victories.

"Behold, I have refined you, but not as silver; I have tried you in the furnace of affliction" (Isaiah 48:10).

"More than that, we rejoice in our sufferings, knowing that suffering produces _____, and endurance produces _____, and character produces _____, and hope does not put us to shame, because God's love has been poured into our hearts through the _____ _____ who has been given to us" (Romans 5:3–5).

"But the _____, the Holy Spirit, whom the Father will send in my name, he will _____ you all things and bring to your remembrance all that I have said to you" (John 14:26).

"Behold, ____ stand at the _____ and _____. If _____ hears my _____ and _____ the _____, I will _____ ____ to him and eat with him, and he with me" (Revelation 3:20).

"No _____ has overtaken you that is not_____ to man. God is _____ and will not let you be _____ beyond your ability, but with the _____He will also _____ the way of _____, that you may be able to _____ it" (1 Corinthians 10:13).

"Count it all _____, my brothers, when you meet _____ of various kinds, for you know that the testing of your faith produces _____. And let steadfastness have its full effect, that you may be _____ and _____, lacking in nothing" (James 1:2–4).

"Today, if you hear his _____, do not _____your hearts" (Hebrews 4:7b).

"I am the _____, and the _____, and the _____; no one comes to the Father, except through _____" (John 14:6).

Do you remember the *gift* mentioned in "Discussion Day Two? We just read in Revelation 3:20 that the Lord stands at the door and knocks, and John 14:6 tells us that Jesus is the *only* way to God. When we open that door for Him to come into our lives, we are accepting the gift He is offering to us. Answer His call. Receive the gift!

"Jesus did not say I am *a* way; He said, I am *the* way. A lot of people think that God is sitting on top of some mountain, and the people of the world have all these different ways to climb up this mountain and get to God who lives on top. They think that it really does not make any difference how they get up to the top where God is because everyone is climbing to get to the same place where they can know God. And so they conclude that any way that they get to the top is fine, or any belief they choose will get them to God. Any path is legitimate because we are all climbing the same mountain, right? Jesus said, 'I am *the* way,' not *a* way, and that is an exclusive statement. If Jesus' words are true, He eliminates all other paths up the mountain to God. If Jesus is the way, the only way that I can come to God, then no one else—not even Mohammed, Confucius, Buddha, or self—is a way to God."[2]

"Jesus is the bridge that brings a holy God and a sinful mankind together. That is why Jesus Christ died. That is why the cross of Christ is the focal point of human history. The New Testament says, 'For there is one God and one mediator between God and men, the man Christ Jesus, who gave himself as a ransom for all men—the testimony given in its proper time' (1 Timothy 2:5)."[3]

How did God speak to you through our Scriptures this discussion day?

_____

_____

_____

_____

"May the God of peace be with you all. Amen" (Romans 15:33).

---

[2] John Maisel, *Is Jesus God?* (East-West Ministries International, 2002), 31–32.

[3] Ibid., 38.

MAKE YOUR FACE SHINE UPON YOUR SERVANT, AND TEACH ME YOUR STATUTES.

PSALM 119:135

PRAY FOR WISDOM, FEAR GOD, AND KEEP HIS COMMANDMENTS

We discussed quite a bit in our last discussion day. Most importantly, we defined *salvation*. We can be judged *not guilty* of our sins if we put our trust in Jesus. We also read about Satan and his attempt to lead us down a path of unrighteousness, and about how we must resist him.

If you have already made the decision to put your trust in Jesus, you know that God promises to be with us always. Stop regularly—whether you're worried, afraid, anxious, stressed, unsure, or sick—and pray. Talk to God. Tell Him you need His strength and wisdom to get through the week, the day, the hour, or the next minute.

"Do _____be _____ about _____, but in everything by _____ and _____ with thanksgiving let your _____ be made known to God" (Philippians 4:6).

Therefore I tell you, _____ _____ ____ _____ about your life, what you will eat or what you will drink, nor about your body, what you will put on. Is not life more than food, and the body more than clothing? Look at the birds of the air: they neither sow nor reap nor gather into barns, and yet your heavenly Father feeds them. Are you not of more value than they? And which of you by being anxious can add a single hour to his span of life? And why are you anxious about clothing? Consider the lilies of the field, how they grow: they neither toil nor spin, yet I tell you, even Solomon in all his glory was not arrayed like one of these. But if God so clothes the grass of the field, which today is alive and tomorrow is thrown into the oven, will he not much more clothe you, O you of little faith? Therefore _____ _____ _____ _____, saying, "What shall we eat?" or "What shall we drink?" or "What shall we wear?" For the Gentiles seek after all these things, and your heavenly Father knows that you need them all. But seek first the kingdom of God and his righteousness, and all these things will be added to you. Therefore ____ _____ _____ _____ about tomorrow, for tomorrow will be anxious for itself. Sufficient for the day is its own trouble. (Matthew 6:25–34)

Can you think of times when the temptation to do wrong was too difficult to ignore? Write those temptations down, and pray for wisdom and guidance to be strong in you when you're faced with them again in the future.

_____

_____

_____

_____

"I can do all things through Him who strengthens me" (Philippians 4:13).

We talked about our spiritual journey in "Discussion Day Three" and about how temptation just may be an opportunity for us to turn away from the wrong choice and consider doing the better thing. We read several Scriptures that told us that trials produce character and endurance, and that when we are afraid we need to put our trust in Jesus.

Have you ever felt, at one time or another, that some trial you were experiencing would never end? I told you that I have felt that way too. We are not alone. Read about the wisest man in the world and what he had to say about life.

And God gave Solomon wisdom and understanding beyond measure, and breadth of mind like the sand on the seashore, so that Solomon's wisdom surpassed the wisdom of all the people of the east and all the wisdom of Egypt. For he was wiser than all other men, wiser than Ethan the Ezrahite, and Heman, Calcol, and Darda, the sons of Mahol, and his fame was in all the surrounding nations. He also spoke 3,000 proverbs, and his songs were 1,005. He spoke of trees, from the cedar that is in Lebanon to the hyssop that grows out of the wall. He spoke also of beasts, and of birds, and of reptiles, and of fish. And people of all nations came to hear the wisdom of Solomon, and from all the kings of the earth, who had heard of his wisdom. (1 Kings 4:29–34)

Solomon wrote in Ecclesiastes 3:1–11a:

For everything there is a season, and a time for every matter under heaven: a time to be born, and a time to die; a time to plant, and a time to pluck up what is planted;

a time to kill, and a time to heal; a time to break down, and a time to build up;

a time to weep, and a time to laugh; a time to mourn, and a time to dance;

a time to cast away stones, and a time to gather stones together;

a time to embrace, and a time to refrain from embracing;

a time to seek, and a time to lose; a time to keep, and a time to cast away;

a time to tear, and a time to sew; a time to keep silence, and a time to speak;

a time to love, and a time to hate; a time for war, and a time for peace.

Scriptures to Consider

"The end of the matter; all has been heard. _____ _____ and keep his _____, for this is the _____ _____ of man. For God will bring every _____ into _____, with every secret thing, whether _____ or_____" (Ecclesiastes 12:13–14). (This was Solomon's conclusion about life.)

"In whom (Christ) are hidden all the treasures of _____ and _____" (Colossians 2:3).

"Therefore, as you received Christ Jesus the Lord, so _____in him, rooted and built up in him and established in the faith, just as you were taught, abounding in _____" (Colossians 2: 6–7).

After Rahab made the decision to follow Yahweh, she said that fellowship with other believers helped her to prosper in her new life. She learned about Yahweh from older, wiser men, and the mature Israelite women taught Rahab how to dress respectfully and keep a home that was pleasing to God and her husband (*Rahab, My Story*, 17–19). Hearing the men and women pray to God for all of their provisions, and thank Him for all of their blessings, Rahab learned to trust Yahweh for all of her needs also. (You can read Proverbs 31 for an understanding of how to be a woman who pleases her husband and God).

After we have made a decision to believe in and follow God, we need to seek out a Bible-teaching church and other believers to learn from and to grow with. If we truly seek God with all our heart and mind, we will be transformed from our former ways and become a new creation.

"My son, if you receive my _____ and treasure up my _____ with you, making your _____ attentive to wisdom and inclining your _____ to _____; yes, if you call out for _____ and raise your voice for _____, if you seek it like silver and search for it as for hidden treasures, then you will understand the _____ of the LORD and find the knowledge of God. For the LORD gives _____; from his mouth come _____ and _____ " (Proverbs 2:1–6).

"Train up a _____ in the way he should go; even when he is _____ he will not _____ from it" (Proverbs 22:6).

"Your _____ is a lamp to my _____ and a light to my _____ " (Psalm 119:105).

"As a deer _____ for flowing streams, so pants my soul for _____, O God" (Psalm 42:1).

Other believers are our spiritual sisters and brothers, and we will spend eternity together as heirs of the kingdom of God!

"And if children, then _____, heirs of God and fellow _____ with _____, provided we _____ with him in order that we may also be _____ with him" (Romans 8:17).

"So that being justified by his grace we might become _____ according to the hope of eternal life" (Titus 3:7).

"Let us hold fast the confession of our hope without _____, for he who promised is _____. And let us consider how to stir up one another to _____ and good works, not neglecting to meet _____, as is the habit of some, but encouraging one another, and all the more as you see the day drawing near" (Hebrews 10:23–25).

Do you remember reading Matthew 7:7–8 in "Discussion Day Two? "Ask, and it will be given to you; seek, and you will find; knock, and it will be opened to you. For everyone who asks receives, and the one who seeks finds, and to the one who knocks it will be opened." Praise God!

You will find many stories of men and women in the Bible who endured trials and tribulations and then went on to praise and thank God for what they learned through the difficult times.

Write your prayer to your heavenly Father, asking to know Him more.

_____

_____

_____

_____

_____

_____

_____

How did God speak to you through our Scriptures this discussion day?

_____

_____

_____

_____

"Therefore, my beloved brothers, be steadfast, immovable, always abounding in the work of the Lord, knowing that in the Lord your labor is not in vain" (1 Corinthians 15:58).

Your word is a lamp to my feet
and a light to my path.

Psalm 119:105

LEARNING TO LIVE FOR GOD

As I awoke this morning, I had glorious thoughts about heaven! A glass-jar candle in my living room displayed many round, sparkling, crystal-like reflections all around the walls and ceiling. (I'm dating myself here, but do you remember the disco days and the mirrored balls in the dance halls?)

As I entered the area, I was enveloped in these gleaming, dancing lights, and I felt so warm and joyful. Wow! Imagine how it will be in the presence of our Lord Jesus, one day, who is the very Light of the World!

In "Discussion Day Four" we learned the importance of gathering together with other believers, learning from their wisdom, and growing in our faith by their examples. We also read what King Solomon said about God: that we are to know Him and obey Him. I'm excited to see what we will discover in "Discussion Day Five."

Isn't God so very loving? He gave us His Word, the Bible, so we could know how to live lives pleasing to Him. Some people say that the letters in *BIBLE* stand for "Basic Instructions Before Leaving Earth."

God didn't leave us, His creation, clueless. We have His Word to guide us in how to live, make righteous decisions, be faithful, act, speak, love, and pray. The Bible teaches us how to trust in the Lord, be saved from our sins, be joyful, and worship Him. The Bible is our precious guidebook.

In chapter seven of *Rahab, My Story*, Rahab said, "Life was easier for me knowing how Yahweh desired me to live. I delighted in knowing what would please the Lord."

We too will delight in knowing that we are pleasing our Lord when we begin to show our good *fruit*.

Scriptures to Consider

"For the _____ all discipline seems _____ rather than _____, but later it yields the peaceful fruit of _____ to those who have been _____ by it" (Hebrews 12:11).

"In the same way, let your _____ shine before others, so that they may see your _____ _____ and give glory to your Father who is in heaven" (Matthew 5:16).

"And so, from the day we heard, we have not ceased to pray for you, asking that you may be filled with the knowledge of his will in all spiritual wisdom and understanding, so as to walk in a manner _____ of the Lord, fully _____ to him, bearing _____ in every good work and increasing in the _____ of God" (Colossians 1:9–10).

"But the fruit of the Spirit is _____, _____, _____, _____, _____, _____, _____, _____, _____-_____; against such things there is no law" (Galatians 5:22).

"By this my Father is _____, that you bear much _____ and so _____ to be my disciples" (John 15:8).

"But now that you have been set free from _____ and have become slaves of _____, the _____ you get leads to _____ and its end, _____ _____" (Romans 6:22).

Rahab learned how to dress respectfully, how to keep a home free from false gods, and how to be a loving wife. She praised Yahweh for forgiving her and for her new life as a believer in Him.

We read in our last discussion day that King Solomon said we must *know* God and obey Him. We need to know more of God's attributes to help us understand Him better. Below is one attribute of our loving Father that we often hear mentioned about Him. Let us try to know and understand the very character of God!

> The *immutability* of God: "God is perpetually the same: subject to no change in His being, attributes, or determinations. Because God has no beginning and no ending, He can know no change."[1]

Arthur W. Pink said the following in the preface of his book, *The Attributes of God*.

> "Something more than a theoretical knowledge of God is needed by us. God is only truly known in the soul as we yield ourselves to Him, submit to His authority, and regulate all the details of our lives by His holy precepts and commandments. 'Then shall we know, if we follow on (in the path of obedience) to know the Lord' (Hosea 6:3). 'If any man will do His will, he shall know' (John 7:17)."[2]

We will look at more attributes of God in each of the following discussion days.

"Now faith is the_____ of things hoped for, the _____ of things not seen" (Hebrews 11:1).

Rahab said that she desired to be obedient and pleasing to the Lord in all she did, said, and thought. She prayed, "Thank You for loving me and for changing my life. I did not think You could love such a sinner as me. How could You forgive all the wicked things I have done in my life? How could You forgive me for worshipping false gods and not running after You? Oh, how could I desire everything but the only One who could truly make me happy? Please forgive me, Lord? Thank you for opening my eyes and heart, and for giving me a life worth living" (*Rahab, My Story*, 13).

I remember a time or season in my life when I spoke to God in a similar way. I was so very thankful that I had come to believe in Him, and I felt grieved thinking of the lifestyle I had been living apart from God. Have you gone through that transition in your life—from living in darkness, completely unaware of our amazing Creator, to a time of

---

[1] Arthur W. Pink, *The Attributes of God* (Baker Books, 1975), 37.

[2] Ibid., preface.

enlightenment or rebirth, fully aware of God and your sinful condition? If so, I know you are so thankful, too.

The only thing to do at that time in my life was to cry out to God, like Rahab did. I didn't know any formal kind of prayer. I simply let my heart speak to the one and only true God of heaven and earth. I asked God to forgive me and to guide me in the way I should go.

If we would only make time daily to read our Bibles, I believe that we, like Rahab, would find life easier, knowing what God expects of us. We would praise God, too, for the promises He has made to give us hope and a future. We would begin to have the foundation of a biblical worldview through which we could filter our thoughts and actions.

Reading through the Scriptures has been like a treasure hunt for me. I have discovered oodles and oodles of treasures—and they weren't even really hidden! Have you experienced the same thing? Isn't it amazing when we read a certain Scripture that we have read several times before and it speaks to us differently? One time that Scripture means one thing to us, and the next time it speaks to us about something completely different. God knows what we need to hear, when we need to hear it, and why we need it for our spiritual growth. God left His instructions (the Bible) for us to read so that we will grow in knowledge, peace, and hope.

We are told that Rahab heard story after story about faithful men like Abraham, Isaac, Jacob, Moses, Joshua, and others—men who, for generations, were faithful to Yahweh. She heard many stories about blessings and punishments, and she was an eyewitness to the complete destruction of Jericho for being a prideful people and worshipping false gods (Joshua 6:20–23).

Rahab said she learned patience from the many stories told about Abraham and Sarah. Abraham told his wife, Sarah, that they needed to wait on the Lord and believe, and that was what they did. It's a good lesson for all of us to learn: we should wait on the Lord and believe. We also read that the Lord's timing is perfect.

"Teach me good judgment and knowledge, for I believe in your commandments" (Psalm 119:66).

Just as Rahab sat listening and learning about Yahweh, we can do the same. Wouldn't you love to be able to sit at the feet of Jesus and listen to Him? How blessed were all of the Lord's disciples to be able to fellowship with Him and be taught by Him. On this side of heaven, we sit in churches or someplace where we can listen to Bible teachings, ask questions, and learn and grow in our faith.

Scriptures to Consider

"_____ in hope, be _____ in tribulation, be _____ in prayer" (Romans 12:12).

"Be _____, therefore, brothers, until the coming of the Lord. See how the farmer waits for the precious fruit of the earth, being _____ about it, until it receives the early and the late rains. You also, be _____. Establish your hearts, for the coming of the Lord is at hand" (James 5:7–8).

"So as to walk in a manner _____ of the Lord, fully _____ to him, bearing _____in every good work and increasing in the _____ of God" (Colossians 1:10).

"_____ are the _____ of the LORD, studied by all who _____ in them" (Psalm 111:2).

"This God—his way is _____; the word of the LORD proves true; he is a _____ for all those who take refuge in him" (Psalm 18:30).

"The law of the LORD is _____, reviving the soul; the testimony of the LORD is _____, making wise the simple; the precepts of the LORD are _____, rejoicing the heart; the commandment of the LORD is _____, enlightening the eyes; the fear of the LORD is _____, enduring forever; the rules of the LORD are _____, and righteous altogether. More to be desired are they than gold, even much fine gold; sweeter also than honey and drippings of the honeycomb" (Psalm 19:7–10).

How did God speak to you through our Scriptures this discussion day?

_____

_____

_____

_____

"The grace of the Lord Jesus be with all. Amen" (Revelation 22:21).

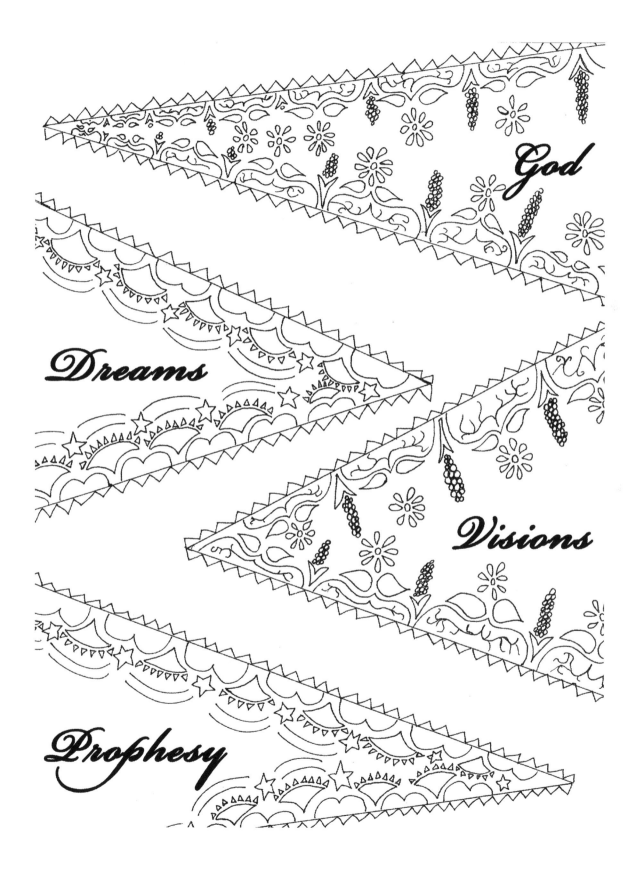

God

Dreams

Visions

Prophesy

DISCUSSION DAY SIX

BORN AGAIN

We had a lot to think about in "Discussion Day Five," didn't we? Hopefully, understanding God's attributes a little more helps us to put things in the right perspective. God is so amazing, great, merciful, holy, supreme, forgiving, and full of grace, and He created *us* to be the focus of His love!

> The *Sovereignty* of God: "Being infinitely elevated above the highest creature, He is the Most High, Lord of heaven and earth. Subject to no one, influenced by no one, absolutely independent; God does as He pleases, only as He pleases, always as He pleases. None can thwart Him, no one can hinder Him. Divine sovereignty means that God is God in fact, as well as in name, that He is on the Throne of the universe, directing all things, working all things after the counsel of His own will."[1]

So, we know we are all sinners; we saw that in "Discussion Day Two" (Romans 3:10–12 and Romans 3:23). We know that God is merciful and full of grace and that He wants us to repent of our sins and turn to Him. When we turn from our sinful nature and begin to change, we become like a new creation, desiring God and His righteousness (2 Corinthians 5:17). Do you remember the good news we read about salvation in "Discussion Day Three"?

Salvation is available to everyone, regardless of a person's color, lifestyle, or sin. We are saved by grace (unearned favor from God), through faith (completely trusting in Christ

---

[1] Arthur W. Pink, *The Attributes of God* (Baker Books, 1975), 32.

and His finished work on the cross). Jesus's death on the cross for our sins makes it possible for us to stand justified before God (not guilty of our sins).

Here is something more for us to think about when we discuss mercy and grace.

> Mercy is when we *don't* receive what we deserve. Grace is when we receive what we *don't* deserve.

We really have to contemplate and meditate on those meanings, don't we?

Rahab's thoughts, concerns, desires, and everything about her were changing. Since putting her complete trust in Yahweh, she was becoming that new person Scripture tells us about.

Scriptures to Consider

> Now there was a man of the Pharisees named Nicodemus, a ruler of the Jews. This man came to Jesus by night and said to him, "Rabbi, we know that you are a teacher come from God, for no one can do these signs that you do unless _____ is with him." Jesus answered him, "Truly, truly, I say to you, unless one is _____ _____ he cannot see the kingdom of God." Nicodemus said to him, "How can a man be born when he is old? Can he enter a second time into his mother's womb and be born?" Jesus answered, "Truly, truly, I say to you, unless one is born of water and the Spirit, he cannot enter the kingdom of God. That which is born of the flesh is _____, and that which is born of the Spirit is _____." (John 3:1–6)

> The *flesh* is described as the source of evil passions and desires; the *spirit* as the source of purity; or as what is agreeable to the proper influences of the Holy Spirit.[2]

"Therefore, if anyone is in _____, he is a _____ creation. The old has _____away; behold, the _____ has come" (2 Corinthians 5:17).

---

[2] Albert Barnes, *Albert Barnes' Notes on the Bible* (1798–1870).

But if some of the branches were broken off, and you, although a wild olive shoot, were grafted in among the others and now share in the nourishing root of the olive tree, do not be arrogant toward the branches. If you are, remember it is not you who support the root, but the root that supports you. Then you will say, "Branches were broken off so that I might be grafted in." That is true. They were broken off because of their _____, but you stand fast through _____. So do not become proud, but fear. For if God did not spare the natural branches, neither will he spare you. (Romans 11:17–21)

Albert Barnes' Notes on the Bible explains Romans 11:17–21 this way:

> "If some of the branches: The illustration here is taken from the practice of those who ingraft trees. The useless branches, or those which bear poor fruit, are cut off, and a better kind inserted. If some of the natural descendants of Abraham, the holy root, are cast off because they are unfruitful, that is because of unbelief and sin."
>
> "Partakes of the root: The in-grafted limb would derive nourishment from the root as much as though it were a natural branch of the tree. The Gentiles derived now the benefit of Abraham's faith and holy labors, and of the promises made to him and to his seed.[3]

A *Christian*, or *disciple*, is a person who believes in and follows Jesus Christ. You could say we are students or pupils of His.

Gentile refers to a person who is not Jewish.

I was a dental assistant for 40 years, primarily in oral surgery. Learning about surgical procedures, sterilization, instruments, X-rays, IV sedation, postoperative care, and working in hospital operating rooms was daunting at times. After much book-studying and several internships, one day things finally clicked! I began to really understand things pertaining to dental assisting. I began thinking like a dental assistant. I began acting like a dental assistant. It was like I was becoming a new or different person. It was as if I had been born again—into a dental assistant's life.

---

[3] Albert Barnes, *Albert Barnes' Notes on the Bible* (1798–1870).

When I was twenty-seven, my husband (boyfriend at that time) and I began reading the Bible for the first time in our lives. We read and read and read. We found a church. We attended Bible studies. We asked questions. And one day things clicked! We realized that we were sinners. We repented of our sins. We asked Jesus to be our Lord and Savior. We were baptized. We listened to wise, mature Christians.

Our heart's desire was to know God. We were baptized as adults, having realized that we were sinners and needed a Savior. We made the decision to accept the gift of salvation offered to us by Jesus. We began to understand that God had a plan for our lives. It was like we were becoming new or different people. We had been born of the flesh (our mothers) when we were infants; now we were born again—spiritually. We began to desire a relationship with God and to read His Word. We wanted to know how to please the Lord and grow in our faith.

Does this make sense? Do you find it all so very exciting? I couldn't contain my enthusiasm when I was spiritually awakened, or *born-again,* and realized that God loved me—me, the sinner, not the good person.

Scriptures to Consider

"And this is the testimony, that God gave us _____ _____, and this life is in his Son. Whoever has the Son _____ _____; whoever does not have the Son of God _____ _____have life. I write these things to you who _____ in the name of the Son of God that you may _____ that you have _____ _____" (1 John 5:11-13).

> Put off your _____self, which belongs to your _____ manner
> of life and is _____ through _____ desires,
> and to be _____ in the spirit of your minds, and to put on the
> _____ _____, created after the likeness of God in true righteousness
> and holiness. Therefore, having put away _____, let each
> one of you speak the _____with his neighbor, for we are members
> one of another. Be angry and do not sin; do not let the sun go down on
> your anger, and give no _____ to the _____. Let
> the thief no longer _____, but rather let him _____, doing
> honest work with his own hands, so that he may have something to share

with anyone in need. Let no _____ talk come out of your _____, but only such as is good for _____ _____, as fits the occasion, that it may give _____ to those who hear. And do not _____ the Holy Spirit of God, by whom you were sealed for the day of redemption. Let all bitterness and wrath and anger and clamor and slander be put_____ from you, along with all malice. Be _____ to one another, tenderhearted, _____ one another, as God in Christ _____you. (Ephesians 4:22–32)

"And I am _____ of this, that he who _____ a good work in you will bring it to _____ at the day of Jesus Christ" (Philippians 1:6).

"The Spirit of the _____ is upon me, because he has anointed me to proclaim _____ _____ to the poor. He has sent me to proclaim _____ to the captives and recovering of _____ to the blind, to set at liberty those who are _____, to proclaim the year of the Lord's favor" (Luke 4:18).

Rahab questioned how God could love her because of the sinful life she had lived. What about God's love for us? What can we do? Can we do good things or perform acts of kindness, and hope that God will look favorably upon us?

Let's finish up today by listing some good or kind things we can do for God, the church, or others, to earn special favor with God.

_____   _____

_____   _____

_____   _____

_____   _____

_____

During our next discussion day we will search the Bible for Scriptures on how God views us as far as being good—and performing good deeds.

How did God speak to you through our Scriptures this discussion day?

_____

_____

_____

_____

"Thanks be to God for his inexpressible gift!" (2 Corinthians 9:15).

GOD KNOWS US INTIMATELY: I DO LOTS OF GOOD DEEDS

We finished up "Discussion Day Six" by listing good or kind things we could do to earn favor with God. Below we will read what Ephesians 2:8–9 has to say about doing those things to earn our way to God. First let us look at another attribute of God.

> God is *love*. "It is not simply that God loves, but that He *is* love itself. Love is not merely one of His attributes, but His very nature. God has loved His people from everlasting, and therefore nothing about the creature can be the cause of what is found in God from eternity."[1]

"Whoever confesses that Jesus is the Son of God, God abides in him, and he in God. So we have come to know and to believe the love that God has for us. God is love, and whoever abides in love abides in God, and God abides in him" (1 John 4:15–16).

"Make your face shine on your servant; save me in your steadfast love!" (Psalm 31:16).

"Many are the sorrows of the wicked, but steadfast love surrounds the one who trusts in the LORD" (Psalm 32:10).

---

[1] Arthur W. Pink, *The Attributes of God* (Baker Books, 1975), 77.

"But I will sing of your strength; I will sing aloud of your steadfast love in the morning. For you have been to me a fortress and a refuge in the day of my distress" (Psalm 59:16).

"For you, O Lord, are good and forgiving, abounding in steadfast love to all who call upon you" (Psalm 86:5).

Let's take a minute to understand our relationship with God a bit more. I want to remind you that God knows our hearts. He knows us intimately. He loves us. He loves us just the way we are.

> O LORD, you have searched me and know me! You know when I sit down and when I rise up; you discern my thoughts from afar. You search out my path and my lying down and are acquainted with all my ways. Even before a word is on my tongue, behold, O LORD, you know it altogether. You hem me in, behind and before, and lay your hand upon me. Such knowledge is too wonderful for me; it is high; I cannot attain it. Where shall I go from your Spirit? Or where shall I flee from your presence? If I ascend to Heaven, you are there! If I make my bed in Sheol, you are there! If I take the wings of the morning and dwell in the uttermost parts of the sea, even there your hand shall lead me, and your right hand shall hold me. If I say, "Surely the darkness shall cover me, and the light about me be night," even the darkness is not dark to you; the night is bright as the day, for darkness is as light with you. For you formed my inward parts; you knitted me together in my mother's womb. I praise you, for I am fearfully and wonderfully made. Wonderful are your works; my soul knows it very well. My frame was not hidden from you, when I was being made in secret, intricately woven in the depths of the earth. Your eyes saw my unformed substance; in your book were written, every one of them, the days that were formed for me, when as yet there was none of them. (Psalm 139:1–16)

"But even the hairs of your head are all numbered" (Matthew 10:30).

Who would do such a thing? We love our families, friends, children, and grandchildren, but have we taken the time to carefully count and caress every hair on their heads? God has!

"You have kept count of my tossings; put my tears in your bottle" (Psalm 56:8).

I sometimes envision walls upon walls of shelves in heaven where the Lord saves tear-filled bottles. I wonder if there is a mansion in heaven called the Mansion of Tears. I imagine that there are small, vial-type bottles on shelves, and that there are some fifty-five-gallon-size tear containers. I know my tears are in the fifty-five-gallon drums—not so much because I am sad so often, but because I am so happy! Most of the tears in the container with my name and picture on it were shed because I am so thankful. They are thankful tears because God loves me, because He has forgiven my sins, because He sent His Son to shed His blood and die for me, and because He has prepared a place for me (Matthew 25:34). How and why He does these things, I don't know. I don't understand it all. I am just so very thankful.

God tells us in Isaiah 55:9, "For as the heavens are higher than the earth, so are my ways higher than your ways and my thoughts than your thoughts." (We read this Scripture when we questioned how God created the earth and everything in it.)

"The LORD is near to the brokenhearted and saves the crushed in spirit" (Psalm 34:18).

If we don't know our Lord and have a relationship with Him, our spirits are crushed. Scripture tells us that God knows us intimately. He loves us. All of our days were planned before even one day was. He created us for His pleasure. He wants our praise, trust, and obedience. He is our loving Father, who desires for us to live life abundantly.

"The thief comes only to steal and kill and destroy. I came that they may have life and have it abundantly" (John 10:10).

Just reading those words puts a smile on my face. How about you? How exciting to think about being happy, secure, and loved. Scripture says to seek God first, before anything else we desire.

Scriptures to Consider

We have read some of these Scriptures before, but they are so significant, let us read them again.

"For _____ have _____ and fall _____ of the glory of God" (Romans 3:23).

"For the _____ of sin is _____, but the _____ gift of God is eternal life in _____ _____ our Lord" (Romans 6:23).

"But God shows his _____ for us in that while we were still _____, Christ _____ for us" (Romans 5:8).

"You did not _____ me, but I _____ you" (John 15:16a).

"For we hold that one is justified by _____ apart from works of the law" (Romans 3:28).

"If you _____ with your mouth that _____ is _____ and believe in your _____ that God raised him from the dead, you will be _____. For with the heart one _____ and is _____, and with the mouth one _____ and is _____" (Romans 10:9–10).

Thinking of the list of our good works we made in "Discussion Day Six", hoping God would view us favorably, how do you think you measure up? I thought I looked pretty darn good when I looked at my list. I have cleaned houses for the elderly, served food at shelters, supervised youth outings, volunteered at schools, brought clothes to shelters, baked for church events, and participated in many outreach programs. That should earn me some points in the *doing good* column of life—or so I thought. You have your list of good works too. Do you think we have earned favor with God, earned our salvation?

Oh, no! Maybe there are others who have done so much more good in life. Is there any hope for us? Or must we do even more good things or good works? When will all of our efforts be good enough?

"For by _____ you have been saved through _____. And this is not your _____ doing; it is the _____ of God, not a result of _____, so that no one may _____" (Ephesians 2:8–9).

We need to read Ephesians 2:8–9 again!

That Scripture mentions the gift of God. What is the gift of God? *Jesus* is the gift, the amazing gift—the good news. Salvation is a gift. We can't earn it. So much for working hard to attain something that is a gift.

When I realized that the Lord was knocking on my heart's door, I opened it to receive forgiveness of sins and the gift of eternal life through our Lord Jesus. Is the Lord knocking at your heart's door? Do you hear the Master's voice?

"The sheep hear his _____, and he calls his own sheep by _____and leads them out. When he has brought out all his own, he goes _____them, and the sheep _____him, for they know his _____" (John 10:3–4).

Remember the list we made of good things we could to do to earn our way to God? How do those good things or good works fit in with God's plan if all the good we do in life doesn't matter? What does God have to say about it?

"You see that a person is justified by works and not by faith alone. And in the same way was not also Rahab the prostitute justified by works when she received the messengers and sent them out by another way? For as the body apart from the spirit is dead, so also faith apart from works is dead" (James 2:24–26).

Because of our faith, we will do good works. Praise God!

We have had so many Scriptures to read and look up each discussion day, I know! But which ones could we leave out?

"All Scripture is breathed out by God and profitable for teaching, for reproof, for correction, and for training in righteousness that the man of God may be competent, equipped for every good work" (2 Timothy 3:16–17).

I encourage you to read biographies of great men and women of faith who performed mighty works by clinging tightly to God and His promises, especially in times of turmoil and trials. Corrie Ten Boom, who was a prisoner in a Nazi death camp, once said that only by looking to Christ could she be at rest. She chose not to focus on her situation, which only distressed her terribly. Rather, she looked to the Lord where she would be comforted. She delighted in her relationship with the Lord.

Don't we desire what she had? Don't we crave rest for our weary souls?

"Come to me, all who labor and are heavy laden, and I will give you rest" (Matthew 11:28).

Are you exhausted from working so hard to have peace and joy in your life? I was. Our own efforts are futile. Let's stop attempting to do what only God can do. Go to Him. Pray to Him. Listen to Him. Know Him. He will give us rest.

How did God speak to you through our Scriptures this discussion day?

_____

_____

_____

_____

"The grace of the Lord Jesus Christ be with your spirit" (Philippians 4:23).

You have kept count
of my tossings; put my
tears in your bottle.
Psalm 56:8

WISDOM AND THE FRUIT OF THE SPIRIT

As we reflected on Corrie Ten Boom's desperate situation our last discussion day, I was convicted of how much I worry about silly little things all of the time. Do you do that too? I continue to ask God for wisdom to grow stronger in my faith and understanding of Him. The Bible is filled with wise guidance for us. Today we will read what God's being *omniscient* means.

God is *omniscient*. Arthur W. Pink writes, "God knows everything: everything possible, everything actual; all events and all creatures, of the past, the present, and the future. He is perfectly acquainted with every detail in the life of every being in heaven, in earth, and in hell. Nothing escapes His notice, nothing can be hidden from Him, and nothing is forgotten by Him."[1]

"_____me, O God, and know my heart! _____me and know my thoughts! And see if there be any grievous way in me, and _____me in the way everlasting!" (Psalm 139:23–24).

"If any of you lacks _____, let him ask _____, who gives _____to all without reproach, and it will be given him" (James 1:5).

---

[1] Arthur W. Pink, *The Attributes of God* (Baker Books, 1975), 17.

"Behold, I am the _____, the God of all flesh. Is anything too _____ for me?" (Jeremiah 32:27).

"And this is eternal life, that they know you, the only true _____, and Jesus Christ whom you have sent" (John 17:3).

So, how do you measure up? After reading Romans 3:23 in our last discussion day, is it clear to you that we all miss the mark? What do we all deserve? Romans 6:23 says we deserve death, but Romans 5:8 says that Jesus died for our sins. Whose sins? Your sins and my sins. Reread John 14:6 and Romans 10:9–10. Then read what Ephesians 2:8–9 tells us.

In spite of our wickedness, in spite of our sinful nature, in spite of all we do, say, and think wrongly, God made a way for us to be with Him, a way to stand before our holy God as sinless. Why? Because He created us as objects of His pleasure, and He desires a relationship with us!

God provided a sacrifice for our sins. Jesus, the Son of God, was born as a baby, lived a sinless life, took *our* sins upon Himself, shed His blood, and died on the cross in our place to *atone* for our sins. He was raised up again, and He lives today, seated at the right hand of God, the Father, to intercede for us. Jesus did it all.

"For there is one God, and there is one mediator between God and men, the man Christ Jesus" (1 Timothy 2:5).

Atonement – "The state of being *at one* or being reconciled. But the word is also used to denote that by which this reconciliation is brought about (the death of Christ itself), and when so used it means satisfaction, and in this sense to make an atonement for one is to make satisfaction for his offenses (Exodus 32:30; Leviticus 4:26; 5:16; Numbers 6:11) and, as regards the person, to reconcile, to propitiate God in his behalf."[2]

You have to ask yourself over and over again: who would do such a thing for us? Why? Even though our finite minds cannot comprehend it, the answer is that God loves us, created us to be objects of His affection, and desires a personal relationship with His

---

[2] M. G. Easton, MA, DD, *Illustrated Bible Dictionary*, 1897.

creation. We keep reading that over and over throughout this discussion guide. Maybe if we read it enough, it will begin to become what we know to be true, because it *is* true!

"For God *so* loved the world [us] that He gave His only son, that whoever believes in Him should not perish but have eternal life" (John 3:16).

"For I am sure that neither death nor life, nor angels nor rulers, nor things present nor things to come, nor powers, nor height nor depth, nor anything else in all creation, will be able to separate us from the love of God in Christ Jesus our Lord" (Romans 8: 38–39).

Rahab wanted to change her ways, but how was she to do it? The two Israelite spies promised to rescue her and her family when Joshua and the Israelites came to attack Jericho (Joshua 2). What would Rahab's life look like as a follower of Yahweh? Would there likely be dramatic changes in her thoughts and actions? When we call out for Jesus to be our Lord and Savior, should we expect changes in our lives?

Scriptures to Consider

"Now the_____ of the _____ are evident: sexual immorality, impurity, sensuality, idolatry, sorcery, enmity, strife, jealousy, fits of anger, rivalries, dissensions, divisions, envy, drunkenness, orgies, and things like these. I warn you, as I warned you before, that those who do such things will _____ inherit the kingdom of God. But the _____ of the _____ is love, joy, peace, patience, kindness, goodness, faithfulness, gentleness, self-control; against such things there is no law" (Galatians 5:19–23).

Rahab came to understand that she and all of Jericho displayed the works of the flesh. Once she came to know Yahweh, her new heart began to display fruits of her new spirit.

"You will _____ them by their_____" (Matthew 7:16a).

Our fruit is how we live our lives. Rahab knew she had changed. She asked her father if he could see changes in her when she went to tell him of a promised rescue in the midst of turmoil in Jericho (*Rahab, My Story*, 60). We will change too. Our hearts will begin to detest the works of the flesh and to desire the works of the Spirit.

"Let no _____ talk come out of your mouths, but only such as is _____ for building up, as fits the occasion, that it may give _____ to those who hear" (Ephesians 4:29).

What is grace? What is sanctification?

> *Grace* is the free and unmerited favor of God, as manifested in the salvation of sinners and the bestowal of blessings.[3]

> *Sanctification* is the act or process of acquiring sanctity, of being made or becoming holy.[4]

After reading the Scriptures we just read in Galatians, Matthew, 2 Corinthians, and Ephesians, I was reminded of a poem my sister Donna once gave to me. It was about a young woman thanking someone in her life for all they had done to teach her life's lessons by their actions. Many instances were mentioned where the young woman witnessed love, respect, care, concern, compassion, responsibility, prayers, and the action taken to demonstrate each—while the exemplary person was unaware of being observed. The poem ended with the young woman thanking the person for all of the lessons she had learned when she witnessed each act of kindness. She said she was now well equipped to be a good, productive person in life!

Imagine impacting someone like that. We've looked at Scriptures saying that people will know who we are by our *fruits* (actions). Do you think that after we repent from our sins and claim Jesus as our Lord and Savior, we might demonstrate the kind of fruit we just read about? I pray that we all display such noble character.

"And let us not grow weary of doing good, for in due season we will reap, if we do not give up" (Galatians 6:9).

"You will recognize them by their fruits. Are grapes gathered from thornbushes, or figs from thistles? So, every healthy tree bears good fruit, but the diseased tree bears bad fruit. A healthy tree cannot bear bad fruit, nor can a diseased tree bear good fruit. Every tree that

---

[3] *Wikipedia Free Encyclopedia*
[4] Ibid.

does not bear good fruit is cut down and thrown into the fire. Thus you will recognize them by their fruits" (Matthew 7:16–20).

Do you see Rahab's life in the Scriptures we just read—before and after she believed in Yahweh? Did her *fruit* change? Did her heart's desire change? Did she begin to change the way she thought and acted? Is it possible that we can do the same thing? Yes!

When we turn from our former ways and become followers of our amazing God, we see things in life differently. We understand the hurt and confusion in others more clearly, because we have been hurt and confused too. We understand that believing in God helps to mend hurts and alleviate confusion. We understand that sometimes hurt people, hurt people. It is a journey we take from sinfulness to faithfulness, from looking through our eyes to looking through the eyes of God, from having a worldly view of things to having a biblical view of things. We experience a transformation that abundantly blesses our lives in many ways and, more importantly, glorifies God.

> Jesus said to them, "I am the bread of life; whoever comes to me shall not hunger, and whoever believes in me shall never thirst. But I said to you that you have seen me and yet do not believe. All that the Father gives me will come to me, and whoever comes to me I will never cast out. For I have come down from heaven, not to do my own will but the will of him who sent me. And this is the will of him who sent me; that I should lose nothing of all that he has given me, but raise it up on the last day. For this is the will of my Father, that everyone who looks on the Son and believes in Him should have eternal life, and I will raise him up on the last day." (John 6:35–40)

In "Discussion Day Twelve" we will be listing family and friends that we pray will come to know our Lord. For now, let's take a minute to list those we don't know very well (and maybe we don't want to know them well) and commit to pray for them to come to know Jesus as their Lord and Savior. An example might be someone like the lady who works at the supermarket cash register who seems sad all of the time. Maybe the grumpy man who pumps your gas needs prayer. Scripture tells us to pray for our leaders. What about an elderly neighbor who lives alone? Your coworkers? Your children's friends? Maybe that person at the playground who told you to learn to keep your kids in order while they were running around, yelling, and having fun—being children! You may have some people in mind who need prayer. List them. Let's pray for them. Don't we really want everyone to know about all of the wonderful promises God has made to those of us who believe in Him?

_____   _____

_____   _____

_____   _____

_____   _____

_____   _____

_____

Scriptures to Consider

"But I say to you, _____ your enemies and _____ for those who persecute you, so that you may be sons of your Father who is in heaven. For he makes his sun rise on the _____and on the _____, and sends rain on the _____ and on the _____. For if you love those who love you, what reward do you have? Do not even the tax collectors do the same? And if you greet only your brothers, what more are you doing than others? Do not even the Gentiles do the same? You therefore must be perfect, as your heavenly Father is perfect" (Matthew 5:44–48).

"But I say to you who hear, _____ your enemies, do _____ to those who hate you" (Luke 6:27).

Jesus was teaching about the final judgment in this next passage.

Then the King will say to those on his right, "Come, you who are blessed by my Father, inherit the kingdom prepared for you from the foundation of the world. For I was hungry and you gave me _____, I was thirsty and you gave me _____, I was a stranger and you _____ me, I was naked and you _____ me, I was sick and you _____ me, I was in prison and you _____ to me." Then the righteous will answer him, saying, "Lord, when did we see you hungry and feed you, or thirsty and give you drink? And when did we see you a stranger and welcome you, or naked and clothe you? And when did we see you sick or in prison and visit you?" And the King will answer them, "Truly, I say to you, as you did it to one of the least of these my brothers, _____ _____ ____ ____ ____" (Matthew 25:34–40).

"Do not neglect to show _____ to _____, for thereby some have entertained _____ unawares" (Hebrews 13:2). How exciting that would be!

How did God speak to you through our Scriptures this discussion day?

_____

_____

_____

_____

"And behold, I am with you always, to the end of the age" (Matthew 28:20b).

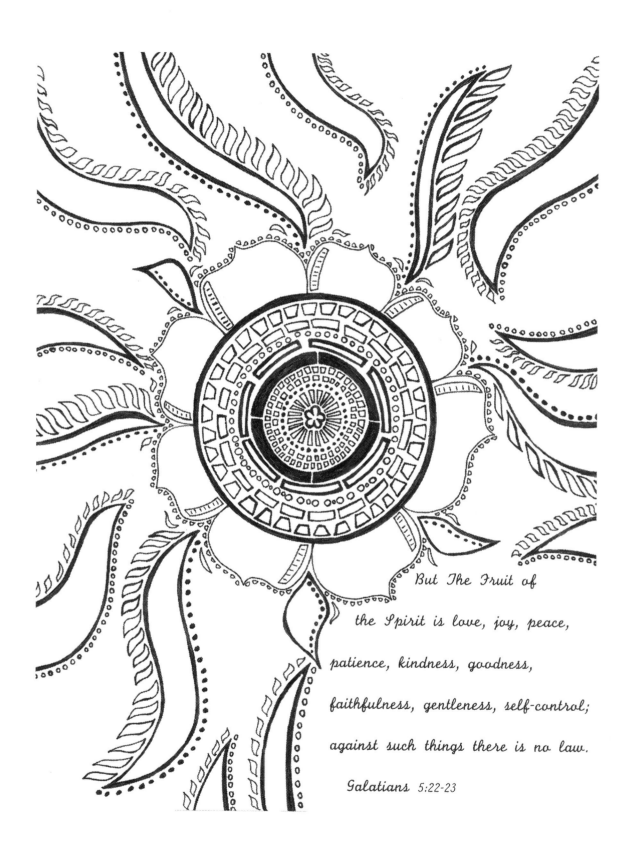

But The Fruit of

the Spirit is love, joy, peace,

patience, kindness, goodness,

faithfulness, gentleness, self-control;

against such things there is no law.

Galatians 5:22-23

FAITHFUL MEN AND GIVING UP CONTROL

I loved thinking about the poem in our last discussion day where the young woman learned so many of life's lessons by observing the woman of virtue. You know, the love you show to others allows them to see Jesus through you. Maybe that is the only Jesus they will ever see. Let's shine!

Are you familiar with this passage of Scripture?

> An excellent wife who can find? She is far more precious than jewels. The heart of her husband trusts in her, and he will have no lack of gain. She does him good, and not harm, all the days of her life. She seeks wool and flax, and works with willing hands. She is like the ships of the merchant; she brings her food from afar. She rises while it is yet night and provides food for her household and portions for her maidens. She considers a field and buys it; with the fruit of her hands she plants a vineyard. She dresses herself with strength and makes her arms strong. She perceives that her merchandise is profitable. Her lamp does not go out at night. She puts her hands to the distaff, and her hands hold the spindle. She opens her hand to the poor and reaches out her hands to the needy. She is not afraid of snow for her household, for all her household are clothed in scarlet. She makes bed coverings for herself; her clothing is fine linen and purple. Her husband is known in the gates when he sits among the elders of the land. She makes

linen garments and sells them; she delivers sashes to the merchant. Strength and dignity are her clothing, and she laughs at the time to come. She opens her mouth with wisdom, and the teaching of kindness is on her tongue. She looks well to the ways of her household and does not eat the bread of idleness. Her children rise up and call her blessed; her husband also, and he praises her: "Many women have done excellently, but you surpass them all." Charm is deceitful, and beauty is vain, but a woman who fears the LORD is to be praised. Give her of the fruit of her hands, and let her works praise her in the gates. (Proverbs 31:10–31)

Wow! What a woman! Let's not measure our strengths against this woman's, but rather let's strive to be thought of as kindly. By loving others, we will be more considerate, thoughtful, and caring toward them. Would you say that we could set goals to be good stewards of all that has been entrusted to us?

Grace is another attribute of God.

Grace is the sole source from which flows the goodwill, love, and salvation of God unto His chosen people." Arthur W. Pink goes on to say that "divine grace is the sovereign and saving favor of God exercised in the bestowment of blessings upon those who have no merit in them and for which no compensation is demanded from them."[1]

Someone might want to know what it is about you that makes you seem so different from others. Someone might ask why you are so joyful, peaceful, and content with life. You will then have an opportunity to share about forgiveness in Christ Jesus and the path to eternity with God, the Father. Oh, to be able to lead others to the life we enjoy in Jesus! We have hope. Share it!

"But in your hearts honor Christ the Lord as holy, always being prepared to make a defense to anyone who asks you for a reason for the hope that is in you" (1 Peter 3:15a).

In chapters 4–8 of *Rahab, My Story*, Rahab heard many stories of faithful men like Isaac, Jacob, Moses, and Joshua by the campfires at night. She heard how Yahweh spoke to Isaac, confirming the promise He had made with his father, Abraham (Genesis 26:3–5).

---

[1] Arthur W. Pink, *The Attributes of God* (Baker Books, 1975), 66.

Rahab also heard this: "One night the Lord spoke to Isaac's son, Jacob, through whom the covenant blessing would be extended. The Lord told Jacob He was the God of Abraham and the God of his father Isaac." Yahweh told Isaac that all the nations of the earth would be blessed because his father, Abraham, obeyed His commandments, statutes, and laws (Genesis 26, 28).

Rahab listened to stories about Moses, the Hebrew who had been brought up as a prince in the palace of Pharaoh (Exodus 2:1–10). She heard that Moses had a heart for his people when he was older, and that he obeyed the Lord when he was told to go to Egypt and lead his people out of captivity to a good and spacious land flowing with milk and honey (Exodus 3).

Later, after Moses died, the Lord used Joshua to complete the task of leading the Israelites into the Promised Land (Joshua 1). The Lord told Joshua that He would be with him and would never leave him. Yahweh told Joshua to "Be strong and courageous!" (Joshua 1:9).

It was during Joshua's time that Rahab met the two spies who promised to rescue her and her family from the total destruction of Jericho (Joshua 2).

Hearing all of those stories about Yahweh taught Rahab of His great might, purpose, and love for His people. Rahab understood more and more of Yahweh's immeasurable greatness when she said, "Surely it is He who commands all things to be."

Rahab witnessed respect, love, and appreciation between Yahweh's people. She said, "Trust and loyalty were not qualities that would describe those of us who lived in Jericho." She also repeatedly expressed how thankful she was that Yahweh had heard her prayers asking to be one of His chosen people.

Along with Abraham, other faithful men such as Isaac, Jacob, Moses, and Joshua obeyed the Lord. God's promises never changed. He spoke the same promises (the covenant) to each one of them that He had spoken to Abraham. Yahweh promised to multiply His chosen people and lead them into the Promised Land ... when the time was right.

The Lord is preparing us for the Promised Land too! Will we be ready?

"But to all who did receive him, who believed in his name, he gave the right to become children of God" (John 1:12).

"Truly, truly, I say to you, whoever hears my word and believes him who sent me has eternal life. He does not come into judgment, but has passed from death to life" (John 5:24).

Have you prayed to ask Jesus to take control of your life? Are you ready to give up control to the One who created you? (Genesis 1:27). The One who knew you before you were even born? (Psalm 139). The One who has counted every hair on your head? (Matthew 10:30). The One who has a plan for your life? (Jeremiah 29:11). The One who will not lose one of His own? (John 6:39). The One who parted the Red Sea for His people? (Exodus 14:21). The One who sent manna from heaven to feed His people? (Exodus 16:4). The One who promised Sarah she would have a baby when she was many years past child-bearing age? (Genesis 17:15–19). The One who created the stars, the sun, the moon, the waters, the animals, fish, and everything? (Genesis 1). The One who promised young Mary that she would have a child who would be the Son of God? (Luke 1:26–32). The One who came to earth to save His people? (Romans 5:6–8). The One who took all of our sins upon Himself, suffered, shed His blood, died on the cross, and was raised again? (1 Corinthians 15:3–5). The one and only true God of heaven above and earth below? The One who is alive today? (Romans 4:25; Acts 2:32).

Scriptures to Consider

"Jesus Christ is the same _____ and _____ and _____ " (Hebrews 13:8).

"For I know the _____ I have for _____, declares the LORD, plans for welfare and not for evil, to give you a _____ and a _____ " (Jeremiah 29:11).

"For it is the LORD your _____ who goes with you. He will not _____ you or _____ you" (Deuteronomy 31:6b).

"He gives _____ to the faint, and to him who has no might he increases _____ " (Isaiah 40:29).

Finally, be _____ in the Lord and in the strength of His might. Put on the _____ armor of God, that you may be able to stand against the schemes of the _____. For we do not wrestle against flesh and blood, but against the rulers, against the authorities, against the

_____ _____ over this present _____,
against the spiritual forces of _____ in the heavenly places. Therefore
take up the whole armor of God, that you may be able to withstand in the
evil day, and having done all, to stand _____. Stand therefore, having
fastened on the belt of _____, and having put on the breastplate of
_____, and, as shoes for your feet, having
put on the _____ given by the gospel of peace. In all
circumstances take up the _____ of faith, with which you can
extinguish all the flaming darts of the _____ one; and take the helmet
of _____, and the sword of the _____, which
is the word of God, praying at all times in the Spirit, with all prayer and
supplication. To that end keep _____ with all perseverance, making
supplication for all the saints. (Ephesians 6:10–18)

"Be _____, and _____ that I am _____. I will be exalted among the
nations, I will be exalted in the earth!" (Psalm 46:10).

"And those who _____ your name put their _____ in you, for you, O LORD,
have not forsaken those who _____ you" (Psalm 9:10).

"O LORD, make me know my end and what is the _____ of my days; let
me know how _____ I am!" (Psalm 39:4).

My prayer for you today is this:

Dear Lord God, we praise you for who You are. Thank You for providing a way for us to
stand before a holy God as not guilty. Please allow each of us to know You are near. Let us
know that You love us and desire to have a relationship with us. Help us to see the world
through Your eyes and understand your plan to lead us down a path of righteousness.
Help us to understand evil and see it for what it is—an attempt by the Evil One to draw
us away from You. Please, God, show us the way to You. Help us to find a place where
we can go to hear the truth, a place where You alone are King, and You alone are praised.
We will be quiet and listen to You.

You may want to write your own prayer to God.

_____

_____

_____

_____

How did God speak to you through our Scriptures this discussion day?

_____

_____

_____

_____

"The grace of our Lord Jesus Christ be with you all" (2 Thessalonians 3:18).

Be strong and courageous. Do not fear or be in dread of them,
for it is the LORD your God who goes with you. He will not leave you or forsake you.
Deuteronomy 31:6

DISCUSSION DAY TEN

DESTINY WITH TWO SPIES, AND CONFIRMATION ABOUT YAHWEH

After realizing that she was not content with her life and that something was missing, Rahab prayed to Yahweh, the God of the Israelites. In simple words she asked Yahweh to forgive her sinful life and to guide her closer to Him and down a path of righteousness. Rahab no longer accepted men to lodge in her home after praying to Yahweh.

Today we need to understand the wrath of God.

The *wrath* of God: Now the wrath of God is as much a divine perfection as is His faithfulness, power, or mercy. It must be so, for there is no blemish whatever, not the slightest defect in the character of God; yet there would be if wrath were absent from Him! The very nature of God makes Hell as real a necessity, as imperatively and eternally requisite, as Heaven. Not only is there no imperfection in God, but there is no perfection in Him that is less perfect than another. The wrath of God is His eternal detestation of all unrighteousness.[1]

Hear the wise counsel from these Scriptures:

"For the LORD your God is a consuming fire, a jealous God" (Deuteronomy 4:24).

---

[1] Arthur W. Pink, *The Attributes of God* (Baker Books, 1975), 82.

"If your right eye causes you to sin, tear it out and throw it away. For it is better that you lose one of your members than that your whole body be thrown into hell. And if your right hand causes you to sin, cut it off and throw it away. For it is better that you lose one of your members than that your whole body go into hell" (Matthew 5:29–30).

> For if God did not spare angels when they sinned, but cast them into hell and committed them to chains of gloomy darkness to be kept until the judgment; if he did not spare the ancient world, but preserved Noah, a herald of righteousness, with seven others, when he brought a flood upon the world of the ungodly; if by turning the cities of Sodom and Gomorrah to ashes he condemned them to extinction, making them an example of what is going to happen to the ungodly; and if he rescued righteous Lot, greatly distressed by the sensual conduct of the wicked (for as that righteous man lived among them day after day, he was tormenting his righteous soul over their lawless deeds that he saw and heard); then the Lord knows how to rescue the godly from trials, and to keep the unrighteous under punishment until the day of judgment. (2 Peter 2:4–9)

"You serpents, you brood of vipers, how are you to escape being sentenced to hell?" (Matthew 23:33).

In chapter 8 of *Rahab, My Story*, Rahab said, "I had begun to consider important things, such as my life and how I should live it, and I thought about the day when I would die." Rahab had many questions. "Is there really a heaven? Is there a place of torment? Is there a God who will judge my life? Will I be held accountable for my actions?"

What do you think about these questions Rahab had?

_____

_____

_____

_____

She also questioned "Could there be a God who forgives sin? A God who can change my life and lead me down a path of righteousness? Does it matter how old I am or how long I have lived such a disobedient life?"

Have you had these same thoughts? What would you say to Rahab's questions?

_____

_____

_____

_____

"If we confess our sins, he is faithful and just to forgive us our sins and to cleanse us from all unrighteousness" (1 John 1:9).

"But these are written so that you may believe that Jesus is the Christ, the Son of God, and that by believing you may have life in his name" (John 20:31).

Eternal things now mattered greatly to Rahab. She stopped purchasing expensive furnishings, clothes, and wines, and now considered her material possessions of little value. She was becoming a changed, or new, person. She was born-again spiritually, now knowing Yahweh and planning to be obedient and to bow down to only Him.

Daily, Rahab tied her drapes back with her scarlet cord to observe activity outside. One day she observed two men amid a group of travelers heading for Jericho's gates. "I squinted, sat straight up, and strained to see off in the distance. I was not sure what it was, but something appeared to be out of the ordinary. Way off, walking amid a group of others, were two men who caught my eye. I'm not sure what it was about them that got my attention, but I was taken with them." Rahab couldn't determine what it was about the two men that had her eyes fixed on them. (*Rahab, My Story*, 52).

Rahab went on to say, "As the men closed in on the city gates, I began breathing heavily. I couldn't help but think wildly about who they could be. Could they possibly be Israelite men, two of Yahweh's chosen people? What would they be doing coming to Jericho? What if they had been sent here to spy out the land?" Rahab had heard that the Israelites had conquered great kings on their journey to Jericho.

Nothing could prevent Rahab from reaching out to Yahweh or to His chosen people.

I understand how Rahab must have felt. When I became a believer, I wanted to run to be with other believers too. I wanted to hear about our Lord—all about Him! I wanted to understand why God had *chosen people*, and why He had spoken to Abraham about a *covenant* and a *promised land*. I wanted to understand why He'd sent His Son to die for my sins, and why He loved me—me, of all people.

I finally did understand that salvation was a gift offered to me by the very God of Abraham, Isaac, and Jacob. That same God loved me too, and the gift of salvation was mine to accept. I didn't have to try to do enough good works to earn my way to God. He had already sent His Son, Jesus, to make a way for me. When our Lord died on the cross, He said, "It is finished." He did the *only* work acceptable to God.

"When Jesus had received the sour wine, He said, 'It is finished,' and He bowed His head and gave up his spirit" (John 19:30).

When some people didn't understand my desire to be in church with other believers to learn and grow in my faith, it was okay with me. They didn't yet understand what I was beginning to understand. We read that Christians display good fruit. I wanted to change into a person who would display good fruit and please my God. It took me years and years to understand the things of God and to understand that His ways are not our ways and that His thoughts are so much higher than our thoughts (Isaiah 55:9). I discovered that to know God was to have a personal relationship with Him; it was not at all about being a religious person. God desires relationships with people, not religions.

Just as Rahab was ready to search for the two men who had entered Jericho's gates, they appeared at her door! When the king's messengers arrived, looking for them moments after they'd entered her home, she hid them under some flax she was drying up on her roof (Joshua 2).

After realizing that the two men were indeed Israelites spying out the land of Jericho, Rahab told them that she knew Yahweh planned to give them the land and that the terror of them was felt by all of Jericho, for they had heard how the Israelites had utterly destroyed two kings east of the Jordan River. She said, "Our hearts have melted and there remains no courage left in any of us." Rahab then professed her faith by proclaiming, "Yahweh is truly God in heaven above and earth beneath" (Joshua 2).

How could Rahab know such things, especially that Yahweh was the only true God?

_____

_____

_____

_____

Jesus said, "No one can come to me _____ the Father who sent me _____ him" (John 6:44a).

Rahab boldly asked the spies to save her and her family when Jericho was attacked, for she had hidden the men from the king's messengers. When the men were finished with their business in Jericho, they left Rahab's home, promising to return and rescue her.

The city gates had been closed, preventing the two spies from exiting through Jericho's gates. Rahab draped her scarlet cord out her window, allowing the men to climb down and escape without being detected. Before they ran off toward the mountains to find safety from the soldiers who were searching for them, the two spies told Rahab to have her scarlet cord hanging out her window so they would recognize her location when they returned to Jericho (*Rahab, My Story*, 55).

It is likely that the two spies shared their faith about Yahweh with Rahab. All believers are to share their faith—the good news!

Scriptures to Consider

"And Jesus came and said to them, "_____ authority in heaven and on earth has been given to _____. Go therefore and make _____ of _____ nations, baptizing them in the name of the Father and of the Son and of the Holy Spirit, _____ them to _____ all that I have _____ you. And behold, I am with you always, to the end of the age" (Matthew 28:18–20).

> *Baptizing* them was an emblem of the purifying influences of the Christian religion through the Holy Spirit, and solemnly devoting them to God.[2]

"He (John the Baptist) came as a _____, to bear witness about the light [Jesus], that all might _____ through him. He was not the light, but came to bear witness about the light" (John 1:7–8).

"After this the Lord appointed seventy-two others and _____ them on ahead of him, two by two, into every town and place where he Himself was about to go. And He said to

---

[2] Albert Barnes, *Albert Barnes' Notes on the Bible*, 1798–1870.

them, 'The harvest is _____, but the laborers are _____. Therefore pray earnestly to the Lord of the harvest to send out laborers into His harvest'" (Luke 10:1–2).

"For _____ who calls on the name of the _____ will be _____. How then will they call on him in whom they have not _____? And how are they to believe in Him of whom they have never _____? And how are they to hear without someone _____? And how are they to preach unless they are _____? As it is written, 'How beautiful are the feet of those who _____ the _____ _____!'" (Romans 10:13–15).

"So faith comes from _____, and hearing through the _____ of Christ" (Romans 10:17).

We read in John 14:6 that Jesus said He was the way, the truth, and the life—the only way to God.

In chapter 10 of *Rahab, My Story*, when the two spies had departed, Rahab said she wanted to run to her father's house immediately to share the good news of Yahweh with them. As it was evening, she had to wait until morning; but as soon as it was light, Rahab set out on her mission! "Hurrying by the guards at the city gates, and ignoring their distasteful comments and whistles, I was fixed on the task before me. Simply looking at the guards who often visited my home made my stomach churn" (*Rahab, My Story*, 58).

Rahab was displaying the fruits of her changing life. She also had wisdom and discernment. She believed the destruction of Jericho was imminent and was amazed at how the men and women of Jericho could be casually going about their normal, everyday tasks.

"As I continued on through the streets, I passed men setting up their displays in the market, several women casually drawing water from a well, and shepherds tending their flocks." Then, after observing two older men bowing down to a large stone statue on a post by the front door of their home, Rahab said, 'I wanted to cry out to them. They are nothing! Stone cannot love you. All of your carved wooden and stone statues cannot protect you and guide you through life. Why have you turned from the God of your ancestors? Why have you shaken your fists in the very face of God? Destroy the evil things, fall on your faces, and beg Yahweh to forgive you before it is too late'" (*Rahab, My Story*, 58).

The changed Rahab could clearly see the sins of her people through her new eyes—people who bowed down to false gods, people who displayed sexual immorality, sorcery, strife, jealousy, fits of anger, rivalries, dissensions, divisions, envy, drunkenness, and orgies. She could see that they were not concerned at all with Yahweh's plan to judge evil and destroy Jericho. They were well pleased to continue living lives far from God.

"And this is the judgment: the light has come into the world, and people loved the darkness rather than the light because their works were evil" (John 3:19).

How did God speak to you through our Scriptures this discussion day?

_____

_____

_____

_____

"Greet one another with the kiss of love. Peace to all of you who are in Christ" (1 Peter 5:14).

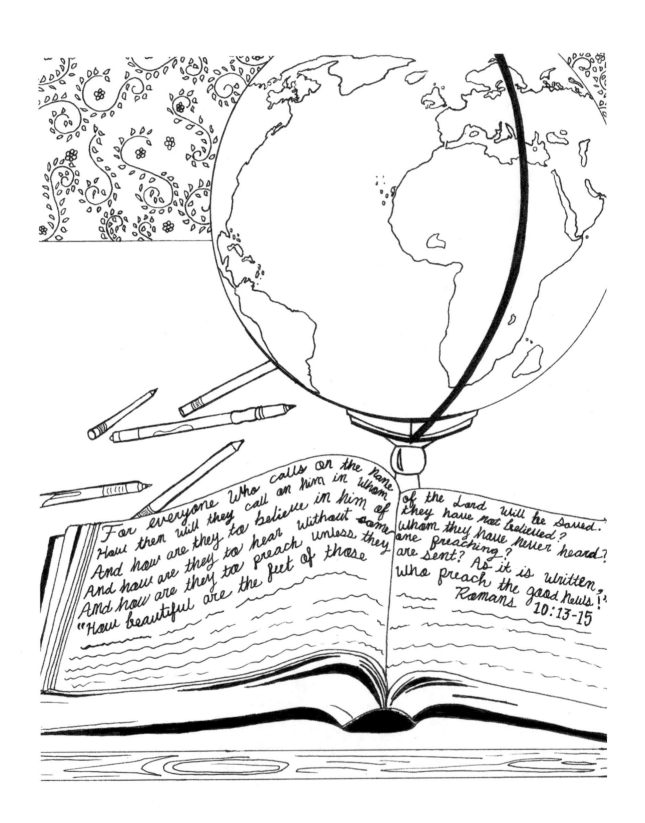

DISCUSSION DAY ELEVEN

EYES OPENED AND HEADING TO THE PROMISED LAND

We read in "Discussion Day Ten" that Rahab professed her faith to the two Israelite spies and that they promised to rescue her and her family when Jericho was attacked. Her eyes were now opened to spiritual things—things of God. "I no longer accepted men for lodging, and I stopped purchasing expensive clothes and wines, which I now deemed of little value; and my thoughts became more deep and meaningful" (*Rahab, My Story*, 48).

I wish I could have been in the room with Rahab and the two spies as they discussed the sovereignty of Yahweh. I would love to have been a witness to Rahab's testimony. I can imagine that Rahab was incredibly thankful and also somewhat confused: thankful that Yahweh would forgive her and have her rescued, and confused about just how God *could* forgive her terrible sins. That is exactly how I felt when I prayed to God to save me. Can you identify with that too?

What did you think when you discovered that Jesus suffered terribly and died for our sins? What might you say to the Lord when you see Him face-to-face one day?

_____

_____

_____

_____

I know what you are thinking. *I need pages and pages to express how thankful I am!* I feel the same way.

This is a good time to look at the mercy of God.

> The *mercy* of God: "The mercy of God has its spring in the Divine goodness. His mercy denotes the ready inclination of God to relieve the misery of fallen creatures. Thus, mercy presupposes sin."[1]

Rahab's life was changed. She diligently observed activity outside her window; for she heard many travelers speak about the Israelite nation camped by the Jordan River. The two spies from Joshua's army had told Rahab that Jericho's days were numbered, and she knew about their plan to attack Jericho. She knew about the covenant between Yahweh and Abraham, and of the promised land Yahweh would give to His people. Though the spies told Rahab they did not know when Jericho would be attacked, she planned to keep watch and be ready for the day of her salvation.

We read that when Rahab observed the two spies walking amid a group of travelers, something about them was different. She was not sure what it was, but the two men were not like the others. Why did they appear to be different?

"What agreement has the temple of God with idols? For we are the temple of the living God; as God said, 'I will make my dwelling among them and walk among them, and I will be their God, and they shall be my people. Therefore go out from their midst, and be separate from them, says the Lord, and touch no unclean thing; then I will welcome you, and I will be a father to you, and you shall be sons and daughters to me,' says the Lord Almighty" (2 Corinthians 6:16–18).

---

[1] Arthur W. Pink, *The Attributes of God* (Baker Books, 1975), 72.

Come out from among them: that is, from among idolaters and unbelievers, from a frivolous and vicious world.

And be ye separate: separate from the world and all its corrupting influences.

And touch not the unclean thing: In Isaiah, "touch no unclean thing" meant that they were to be pure and to have no connection with idolatry in any of its forms. So Christians were to avoid all unholy contact with a vain and polluted world.

And I will receive you: That is, I will receive and recognize you as my friends and my adopted children. This could not be done until they were separated from an idolatrous and wicked world. The fact of their being received by God and recognized as His children depended on their coming out from the world.[2]

"So it will be at the close of the age. The angels will come out and _____ the _____ from the _____" (Matthew 13:49).

"Before him will be gathered all the nations, and he will _____ people one from another as a _____ separates the _____ from the _____" (Matthew 25:32).

Rahab was filled with abundant joy! She had made the decision to follow Yahweh, and her heart was His. She separated herself from the men who used to lodge at her home and from the evil worship of false gods that lurked in Jericho. She shared her newfound faith with her family, and she told them what they must do to be saved.

"The very moment you hear that the Israelite people are coming to attack Jericho, you must come quickly to my home. Travel lightly; take only what is necessary. Make haste, and stop for no one" (*Rahab, My Story*, 60).

Rahab understood that it was urgent for her family to make a decision to follow Yahweh, for no one knows the hour when our Lord will return for His people. You and I must be ready also.

"But concerning that day and hour _____ _____ _____, not even the angels of heaven, nor the Son, but the _____ only" (Matthew 24:36).

---

[2] Albert Barnes, *Albert Barnes' Notes on the Bible* (1798–1870).

"Then will appear in heaven the sign of the Son of Man, and then all the tribes of the earth will mourn, and they will see the Son of Man coming on the clouds of heaven with _____and great_____. And he will send out his _____with a loud trumpet call, and they will _____his elect from the four winds, from one end of heaven to the other" (Matthew 24:30–31).

"He said to them, 'It is not for you to know _____ or _____that the Father has fixed by His own authority'" (Acts 1:7).

"Then the King [Jesus] will say to those on his right, 'Come, you who are _____ by my Father, _____the kingdom prepared for you from the foundation of the world'" (Matthew 25:34).

Rahab would be rescued along with her family. She had hope and a future. She prayed often to Yahweh, thanking Him for caring about someone like her. Rahab was so thankful for God's undeserved mercy.

I remember one day when I was twenty-seven and profoundly unhappy. After reading in the Bible that God loved me and promised to give me rest, hope, and a future, I prayed to Him and asked for His help and guidance.

After Rahab had heard the many stories of Yahweh and the love He had for His people, she prayed to Him. She asked for God's help. I feel something of a kindred spirit with Rahab. All believers are sisters and brothers in Christ. We are all part of one family—God's family.

Are you in a season of your life where you feel like you have no one to turn to for help? No one you feel safe with or can trust? No one who will forgive you? I pray that our past several discussion days have directed your path to the One you *can* trust in, the One who wants to heal your hurts, forgive your sins, and prepare a place for you in heaven.

Don't wait. No special prayer is needed to speak to our heavenly Father. Just pray to Him from your heart. He made us. Remember that He knit us together in our mother's womb (Psalm 139:13). His eyes saw our unformed substance. Our days were planned before even one came to be. He knows us. He loves us. He knows our requests before we even ask Him! Kneel before the Lord and cry out to Him. Fall into His arms. He wants to forgive you, love you, and care for you. If you choose to, write out what you want to say to our Lord. Acknowledge your sins, repent, and trust in Jesus. Ask for forgiveness and guidance and change into the person God wants you to become.

_____

_____

_____

_____

_____

_____

_____

_____

_____

Scriptures to Consider

"Let us then with confidence draw _____ to the throne of _____, that we may receive _____ and find _____ to help in time of need" (Hebrews 4:16).

"_____ without _____" (1 Thessalonians 5:17).

"And I will give you a _____ heart, and a _____ spirit I will put within you. And I will remove the heart of _____ from your flesh and give you a heart of _____" (Ezekiel 36:26).

"Do not be _____ to this world, but be _____ by the renewal of your mind, that by testing you may discern what is the will of God, what is _____ and _____ and _____" (Romans 12:2).

> Put on then, as God's chosen ones, holy and beloved, _____ hearts, kindness, humility, meekness, and patience, _____ with one another and, if one has a complaint against another, _____ each other; as the Lord has _____ you, so you also must _____. And above all these put on _____, which binds everything together in _____ harmony. And let the _____ of Christ rule in your hearts, to which indeed you were called in one body. And be _____. Let the word of Christ dwell in you richly, teaching and admonishing one another in all wisdom, singing psalms and hymns and spiritual songs, with _____ in your hearts to God. And whatever you do, in word or deed, do everything in the name of the Lord Jesus, giving _____ to God the Father through him. (Colossians 3:12–17)

Our church family desires to be a comfort to us in times of trials. Let's review Galatians 6:1–2: "Brothers, if anyone is caught in any transgression, you who are spiritual should restore him in a spirit of gentleness. Keep watch on yourself, lest you too be tempted. Bear one another's burdens, and so fulfill the law of Christ."

We can change. I couldn't change alone. Rahab said she couldn't change alone. She and I both knew we needed help. We both called out to God, and He was there. He always was and always will be.

Yahweh loved Rahab and guided her into a relationship with Him. God loved me and guided me into a relationship with Him. God is waiting for you to accept Him as your Lord and Savior so He can guide you into a relationship with Him. Go to the cross and leave your fears, tears, and hurts there. Jesus died to set us free. Trust in the only one who can fill all of our desires and needs, set the captives free, and mend our broken hearts.

"The Spirit of the Lord is upon me, because he has anointed me to proclaim _____ _____ to the _____. He has sent me to proclaim _____ to the captives and recovering of _____ to the blind, to set at _____ those who are oppressed, to proclaim the year of the Lord's favor" (Luke 4:18–19).

"And those who _____ your name put their _____ in you, for you, O LORD, have not _____ those who seek you" (Psalm 9:10).

Jesus came to set the captives free. What has you imprisoned? When you surrender to Jesus, you will receive a new heart, and you will be a new creature *so* loved by God.

Another acronym to think about is PUSH: Pray Until Something Happens!

How did God speak to you through our Scriptures this discussion day?

_____

_____

_____

_____

"But grow in the grace and knowledge of our Lord and Savior Jesus Christ. To him be the glory both now and to the day of eternity. Amen" (2 Peter 3:18).

Put on then, as God's chosen ones, holy and beloved, compassionate hearts, kindness, humility, meekness, and patience, bearing with one another and, if one has a complaint against another, forgiving each other; as the Lord has forgiven you, so you also must forgive. And above all these put on love, which binds everything together in perfect harmony. Colossians 3:12-14

COME, LORD!: THE WRATH OF GOD

Our God is to be praised! No one compares with Him.

> *The holiness of God*: "He is so because the sum of all moral excellency is found in Him. He is absolute purity."[1]

It is difficult to compute such a magnitude of greatness as we learn the very character of God, isn't it?

Rahab was excited, thankful, and humbled; Yahweh would have her saved. He heard her prayers and answered them. She couldn't think of anything else that mattered but to be ready for the day when the two spies from Joshua's army would return to rescue her and her family.

Although she did not know when that would be, Rahab decided to live only to please Yahweh from that time on. Rahab knew with all of her heart that Yahweh was indeed the only true God of heaven above and of the earth below. She was staking her claim to be at His feet and would allow Yahweh to guide her path from then on. Shouldn't we do the same?

Remember Psalm 119:105? "Your word is a lamp to my feet and a light to my path."

---

[1] Arthur W. Pink, *The Attributes of God* (Baker Books, 1975), 41.

Rahab began to see how far she and the people in Jericho had strayed from God. They worshipped false gods, and they had all been consumed with sin, lust, and money. She also said she understood that death would be a just punishment for sin. *"How could one offend God Almighty and not think there would be judgment one day? she wondered"* (*Rahab, My Story*, 65).

"For we must all appear before the judgment seat of Christ, so that each one may receive what is due for what he has done in the body, whether good or evil" (2 Corinthians 5:10).

Are you able to see how mankind has strayed from God's plan for our lives? In what ways?

_____

_____

_____

_____

We read earlier in Romans 3:23 that we all have sinned. We oftentimes place more importance on material things, people, or events rather than to seek God first in our lives.

In chapter 12 of *Rahab, My Story*, Rahab said that she was sitting by her window one day, looking out and anticipating her rescue, when she noticed smoke off in the distance. "I couldn't see any fires. Wait, not smoke, but dust. Dust was rising into the air and swirling around as if to make some sort of announcement" (*Rahab, My Story*, 68).

The Israelites had begun their march toward Jericho. "Is this the day, Lord?" she wondered. Her faith had increased, and she anxiously awaited her rescue. Rahab prayed for her family to arrive at her door. "It would be as if they were knocking on your door, Lord. Knock, and it shall be opened; seek, and you shall find" (*Rahab, My Story*, 69). "Please have my family be seeking you with all of their hearts." She had shared her new faith with them. "Decide whom you will serve. If you say yes to Yahweh, bend your knee to only Him and turn from your wicked ways, and seek to please God."

Rahab asked Yahweh to come soon. She wanted to belong to Him, to love, praise, trust, and serve Him. Rahab knew she couldn't *make* her family believe and trust in Yahweh. All she could do was pray for them. The rest would be up to Yahweh and each individual.

Does your family know the Lord? What about your friends? Do you desire mercy, grace, hope, and salvation for their lives? Write the names of those you pray will come to know the Lord. Commit to bring them before the Lord in prayer.

_____

_____

_____

_____

_____

_____

When the battle for Jericho began, all of Rahab's family eventually did arrive at her door to be rescued by the two spies. Did they make a true decision for God, or were they just looking for temporary safety? Only God knows, for only He can judge hearts and true motives.

"You know when I sit down and when I rise up; you discern my thoughts from afar. You search out my path and my lying down and are acquainted with all my ways. Even before a word is on my tongue, behold, O LORD, you know it altogether" (Psalm 139:2–4).

"Prove me, O LORD, and try me; test my heart and my mind" (Psalm 26:2).

After anxiously observing the Israelite army march around Jericho that first day without attacking and then retreating back to their camp, Rahab worried some, but she believed the promise the spies had made to rescue her. As the Israelites marched away from Jericho back toward the Jordan River, Rahab prayed, "Lord, come back! Do not forsake me." Rahab wanted to be with the Lord (*Rahab, My Story*, 71–73).

Her family, on the other hand, did not have the same faith and wanted to return to their homes, to their former ways. Growing in her faith, Rahab announced to her family, "The Lord will provide for us. His spies have made an oath to rescue us, so we will be protected and provided for by the Lord. We must trust in Yahweh."

Rahab recounted the many miracles she'd heard that the Lord had performed for His people throughout the generations. Everything He had purposed was meant to carry out the promise made to His servant Abraham long ago. She told her family that the Israelite nation would indeed conquer and possess Jericho—just not that night. The book of Joshua in the Old Testament tells of the attack on Jericho.

> "On the seventh day they rose early, at the dawn of day, and marched around the city in the same manner seven times. It was only on that day that they marched around the city seven times. And at the seventh time, when the priests had blown the trumpets, Joshua said to the people, 'Shout! For the LORD has given you the city. And the city and all that is within it shall be devoted to the LORD for destruction. Only Rahab the prostitute and all who are with her in her house shall live, because she hid the messengers whom we sent'" (Joshua 6:12–17).

The attack on Jericho had begun! Rahab said, "I looked out my window to see stones falling from the wall and everything around us shifting. We held the children tightly, not knowing if we should flee the tumbling structure or wait. Things were breaking and crashing to the ground all around us. My brothers were gathering their children to get them to safety—if there was safety anywhere to be found. I tried to speak over the unthinkable noise, frantically attempting to gather my family together and keep them inside my home, but one of my brothers pulled away from me and went toward the door, his family in tow." Rahab cried out to her brother, "You must not leave. Come back. Stay inside! Please!"(*Rahab, My Story*, 77).

We all have to make those choices: stay strong and trust in God, or go back to our former ways. Do you remember that God said He will never leave us or forsake us? Let's not trust in God just when things are going smoothly in our lives. Don't run away from God when trials come that frighten and confuse us. Run to Him! Seek shelter in Him—the only safe place.

"Let me dwell in your tent forever! Let me take refuge under the shelter of your wings!" (Psalm 61:4).

"And behold, I am with you always, to the end of the age" (Matthew 28: 20b).

"Count it all joy, my brothers, when you meet trials of various kinds, for you know that the testing of your faith produces steadfastness. And let steadfastness have its full effect, that you may be perfect and complete, lacking in nothing" (James 1:2–4).

Albert Barnes' Notes on the Bible has this to say about James 1:2–4.

> The meaning of this is explained in the following phrase - "wanting nothing;" that is, that there may be nothing lacking to complete your character. There may be the elements of a good character; there may be sound principles, but those principles may not be fully carried out so as to show what they are. Afflictions, perhaps more than anything else, will do this, and we should therefore allow them to do all that they are adapted to do in developing what is good in us.[2]

As promised, the spies returned, saw Rahab's scarlet cord hanging out of her window on the wall of Jericho, and rescued her and her family. As the spies led them all out through unthinkable horror and destruction, nothing looked familiar to Rahab. They were not sure of their footing. Rahab asked, "Where are the city gates and the indestructible walls of Jericho? Where is the well I would visit daily for my water?" (*Rahab, My Story*, 78).

Rahab saw soldiers who used to visit her sprawled on the ground! She thought, "Didn't they know death would be a consequence of their disobedience?"

Beginning to understand the attributes or character of God, do you think Rahab's statement about consequences for disobedience sounded harsh?

_____

_____

_____

_____

Back in "Discussion Day Ten" we read about the wrath of God. Let's review it again.

---

[2] Albert Barnes, *Albert Barnes' Notes on the Bible* (1798–1870).

The *wrath* of God: Now the wrath of God is as much a divine perfection as is His faithfulness, power, or mercy. It must be so, for there is no blemish whatever, not the slightest defect in the character of God; yet there would be if wrath were absent from Him! The very nature of God makes Hell as real a necessity, as imperatively and eternally requisite, as Heaven. Not only is there no imperfection in God, but there is no perfection in Him that is less perfect than another. The wrath of God is His eternal detestation of all unrighteousness.[3]

The Israelites conquered Jericho as the Lord had planned hundreds of years earlier. As the two spies guided Rahab and her family to safety, Rahab's heart clung to Yahweh. She prayed as she ran, asking Yahweh, "Carry me along, Lord, for I cannot survive this on my own. I am weak and you are strong; be my shield." She realized she was leaving everything behind—or nothing.

"May the LORD answer you in the day of trouble! May the name of the God of Jacob protect you! (Psalm 20:1).

"The LORD is my strength and my shield; in Him my heart trusts, and I am helped; my heart exults, and with my song I give thanks to Him" (Psalm 28:7).

When our time comes to leave for the promised land, will we worry about what we are leaving behind? I think not! When I was spiritually awakened, or born-again, I just focused on the Lord as Rahab did. I ran to my future with God, gladly leaving behind everything of this world.

Run into His arms. Don't continue to chart your own course. Leave behind heartache, pain, sorrow, lies, confusion, disappointments, discouragements, grief, loss, and death. Really, what would we miss of this world when God has promised us that He has prepared a place for us where there will be no more pain or suffering, a place where we will live with Him?

"He will wipe away every tear from their eyes, and death shall be no more, neither shall there be mourning, nor crying, nor pain anymore, for the former things have passed away" (Revelation 21:4).

---

[3] Arthur W. Pink, *The Attributes of God* (Baker Books, 1975), 82.

"In my Father's house are many rooms. If it were not so, would I have told you that I go to prepare a place for you?" (John 14:2).

Earth is not our home! We are just passing through.

"Yet you do not know what tomorrow will bring. What is your life? For you are but a mist that appears for a little time and then vanishes" (James 4:14).

Scriptures to Consider

"For the one who sows to his own flesh will from the flesh reap_____ , but the one who sows to the Spirit will from the Spirit reap _____ _____" (Galatians 6:8).

"But one thing I do: _____what lies _____and straining _____to what lies ahead. I press on toward the goal for the _____of the upward call of God in Christ Jesus" (Philippians 3:13b–14).

"Though you have not _____ Him, you _____ Him. Though you do not now _____ Him, you _____ in Him and rejoice with joy that is inexpressible and filled with glory, obtaining the outcome of your faith, the salvation of your souls" (1 Peter 1:8–9).

"Therefore, we are ambassadors for Christ, God making His appeal through us. We _____ you on behalf of Christ, be _____ to God" (2 Corinthians 5:20).

As Rahab ran to Yahweh, she again had questions. "How could we have not known there would be judgment one day? Did we think we could just go on living outside of God's laws and not be held accountable, not face punishment? How did you put up with our reckless lifestyle for so long, Lord?" (*Rahab, My Story*, 80).

Are we deserving of punishment if we have lived apart from God? Are there consequences for our actions? Are we held accountable for our actions? We reviewed the wrath of God a bit earlier and again read that God's wrath is as much a perfection of God's divine character as is His faithfulness, power, or mercy. Is punishment just?

_____

_____

_____

_____

Rahab experienced a dramatic change, escaping from utter destruction and horror to approaching Yahweh's people where she could sense peace, contentment, and joy. We are promised peace, contentment, and joy—even through our trials in life (James 1:2)—when we make a decision to turn from our sinful ways and acknowledge God and His perfect plan for our lives!

How does God treat us when we turn to Him and ask for forgiveness?

_____

_____

_____

_____

"They show that the work of the law is written on their _____, while their conscience also bears_____, and their conflicting thoughts accuse or even excuse them on that day when, according to my gospel, God judges the secrets of men by Christ Jesus" (Romans 2:15–16).

"If my people who are called by my name _____ themselves, and _____ and seek my face and _____ from their wicked ways, then I will _____ from heaven and will _____ their sin and _____their land" (2 Chronicles 7:14).

"And no longer shall each one teach his neighbor and each his brother, saying, 'Know the LORD,' for they shall all know me, from the least of them to the greatest, declares the LORD. For I will _____ their _____, and I will remember their sin ____ _____" (Jeremiah 31:34).

"For if you _____ others their trespasses, your heavenly Father will also _____you, but if you do not forgive others their trespasses, neither will your Father forgive your trespasses" (Matthew 6:14–15).

"And whenever you stand praying, _____, if you have anything against anyone, so that your Father also who is in heaven may _____you your trespasses" (Mark 11:25).

"If we _____ our sins, he is faithful and just to _____ us our sins and to cleanse us from all _____" (1 John 1:9).

How did God speak to you through our Scriptures this discussion day?

_____

_____

_____

_____

"Now to him who is able to keep you from stumbling and to present you blameless before the presence of his glory with great joy, to the only God, our Savior, through Jesus Christ our Lord, be glory, majesty, dominion, and authority, before all time and now and forever. Amen" (Jude vv. 24–25).

NOW YOU KNOW

You have probably heard people talk about being lost for a time and then being found—being blind, but then being able to see. They are speaking about their lives *before* they came to know the Lord, and their lives *after* coming to know Him.

That was me. That was Rahab. How about you? I could cry fountains of joyful tears. I am found. I am thankful. I know Jesus died for my sins, but I still can't believe it. How could anyone die for all of my wretched sins? I often think, *Why Lord? Why me?* I have to remind myself that we were created as objects of God's affection, and that because God forgives me through Christ, I need to accept His forgiveness.

Don't look in the rearview mirror and lament over past sins. Be thankful. Know God and make Him known.

At a point or season in time, Rahab recognized that she was not content with her life. Remember Ecclesiastes 3:1–11a? "For everything there is a *season*, and a *time* for every matter under heaven."

Rahab heard stories about the only true God and the love He had for His people. Her heart desired to know God, and she was convicted of her sinful lifestyle. She truly sought to change her ways.

Remembering the destruction of Jericho, Rahab said, "Those of us living there were disobedient to Yahweh and suffered the just consequences. We were punished for our refusal to worship only Yahweh and put aside all others." She also said, "I saw the temples tumble into piles of rocks, the priests running with no place to hide, and many kneeling to pray, but those prayers came too late!"(*Rahab, My Story*, 34).

Rahab prayed to God and asked for forgiveness, wisdom, and guidance. She was born-again spiritually and became a new believer in Yahweh. Her life was about to have meaning and purpose, and God would guide her steps. "Your word is a lamp to my feet and a light to my path" (Psalm 119:105).

Fleeing from Jericho, Rahab reached her heart's desire: Yahweh and His chosen people. "We put great distance between ourselves and Jericho. The sounds of death began to fade away, and we began to slow down our frantic pace. Wiping dust and tears from my face and eyes, I tried to focus on what was before me. The horrible screeching and confusion all around us was taken over in my mind by an approaching incredible sight. There before me, getting closer and closer, stood a great multitude, the chosen people, the children of God! It was as if I had been given a glimpse into heaven and was trespassing on sacred ground!" (*Rahab, My Story*, 81).

Yahweh guided Rahab to His people—her people now. Rahab's prayers were answered. She acknowledged that her life would be very different now, but she was not filled with fear by that thought. She was content, thankful, and joyful. She was with Yahweh and His people, and that was all that really mattered to her. She would trust Yahweh completely for all of her needs. "Search me, Lord, and know my thoughts," Rahab prayed. "Teach me to avoid anything that offends You, and don't let me wander from Your commands. I have chosen to be faithful."

"There is no _____in love, but perfect love casts out _____. For fear has to do with punishment, and whoever fears has not been perfected in love" (1 John 4:18).

Rahab shared those thoughts with her family and told them that they had to make their own decision to follow God. She realized that the rest would be between them and God. The gifts of mercy, grace, and salvation she had accepted from Yahweh were offered to her family also. The gifts of mercy, grace, and salvation are offered to us too. Claim them!

Why is it that when people make a decision to accept Jesus as Lord and Savior, they (including me) want to clean up their lives first? When we recognize our sinful and lost condition, we don't want it exposed for anyone to see. Our heart is convicted of our sins, and we feel ashamed.

I was thinking about this, and something came to mind. My family runs a car wash business. You know, the kind of car wash where you stay in your vehicle and the conveyor pulls your car slowly through the wash. You experience the water spray; colorful, scented soap; swishing sponge cloths; flashing lights; undercarriage spray; wax spray; the rinse; and finally, the drying. You probably vacuum your vehicle before or after your wash, purchase your favorite air freshener, and maybe apply tire shine—all to have a beautiful, shiny, clean car.

Isn't that what we consider doing with our lives? We plan to work on ourselves to get all clean and shiny, and then as our clean car exits the car wash, we will open the passenger door and invite Jesus into our lives.

This sounded like a good plan to me. I didn't want Jesus to see the filth in my life. No way! I didn't want Him to know all the ugly truths about my life—as if He wasn't the one who had created me and already knew every single thing about me from my very beginning through eternity.

"But God shows his _____ for us in that while we were still _____, Christ _____ for us" (Romans 5:8). This occurred *while we were sinners*, not after we've attempted to clean up our lives.

As I read the Bible, asked questions, and grew in my faith, I realized that Jesus wants us to slide over into the passenger seat *immediately* and allow Him to be the driver, the one in control! *He* wants to wash us clean. Indeed, we were washed clean by His shed blood on the cross. He has a plan, and His plan is perfect, so let's let go of our pride and allow the one who created us and knew us before we were even formed have control and be Lord of our lives.

"For I know the plans I have for you, declares the LORD, plans for welfare and not for evil, to give you a *future* and a *hope*" (Jeremiah 29:11). We can never read this Scripture too much!

How incredible is our God!

After following the customs and laws of the Israelite people, Rahab married, grew in her faith, and had a child named Boaz. She grew in her faith by hearing the older men tell stories of Yahweh passed down through the generations. There was no printed Bible in the time that Rahab lived. People orally recounted stories of all the mighty works and wonders God had performed throughout time.

How can we grow in our faith? That is such an important question. In "Discussion Day Four" we talked about not forsaking our gathering together.

"Let us hold fast the confession of our hope without wavering, for he who promised is faithful. And let us consider how to stir up one another to love and good works, not neglecting to meet together, as is the habit of some, but encouraging one another, and all the more as you see the Day drawing near" (Hebrews 10:23–25). Search for a Bible-teaching church. Seek out other believers.

What about our talk? Our actions?

Here we read about works of the *flesh* (before we become believers). "Now the *works of the flesh* are evident: sexual immorality, impurity, sensuality, idolatry, sorcery, enmity, strife, jealousy, fits of anger, rivalries, dissensions, divisions, envy, drunkenness, orgies, and things like these. I warn you, as I warned you before, that those who do such things will not inherit the kingdom of God. [As believers and new creations we will want to distance ourselves from the works of the flesh and begin to display new fruit.] But the *fruit of the Spirit* is love, joy, peace, patience, kindness, goodness, faithfulness, gentleness, and self-control" (Galatians 5:19–23, emphasis added).

Right now you know everything you need to know to cry out to God. You don't need to clean up your life first. He will clean it like we can't even imagine. He will make us amazing vessels that will shine His light through our lives for others to see. We will walk with our heads held high, knowing that: "He who is in you is greater than he who is in the world" (1 John 4:4b).

Greater is he that is in you, than he that is in the world. God, who dwells in your hearts, and by whose strength and grace alone you have been enabled to achieve this victory, is more mighty than Satan, who rules in the hearts of the people of this world, and whose seductive arts are seen in the efforts of these false teachers. The apostle meant to say that it was by no power of their own that they achieved this victory, but it was to be traced solely to the fact that God dwelt among them, and had preserved them by his grace. What was true then is true now. He who dwells in the hearts of Christians by his Spirit, is infinitely more mighty than Satan, "the ruler of the darkness of this world"; and victory, therefore, over all his arts and temptations may be sure. In his conflicts with sin, temptation, and error, the Christian should never despair, for his God will insure him the victory.[1]

Rahab always prayed to God. She knew she needed to be close to Him. She wanted to be close to where she could hear about God. She sat by the campfires at night, listening to stories about God. She asked her husband, Salmon, to tell her stories about God. She prayed to God daily with the Israelite women by the well. She prayed to God about her family. She prayed for the needs of others. She prayed and prayed and prayed. Communication with Yahweh was first in Rahab's life.

We must seek God first. "But seek first the kingdom of God and His righteousness, and all these things will be added to you" (Matthew 6:33).

Do you remember what was important to Rahab when she lived in Jericho, before she knew Yahweh?

_____

_____

_____

After Rahab was born-again spiritually and became a believer, what was important to her?

_____

_____

_____

_____

---

[1] Albert Barnes, *Albert Barnes' Notes on the Bible* (1798–1870).

In "Discussion Day One", after reading about what Rahab deemed important to her before she became a believer in Yahweh, we listed things that were important to us—things that we gave most of our attention to. What do you think about those things now? Do you feel differently? If you were to rewrite your list, what would it look like now?

_____

_____

_____

_____

_____

My list changed dramatically after I asked Jesus into my life. I realized that the things I thought I needed were material things. As I grew in my faith, I realized that all I really needed was our great, amazing God. Everything else would fall into place after that.

As Rahab considered all things pertaining to Yahweh, she remembered the stories of the many plagues Egypt had endured when Pharaoh had refused to let the Israelite people go so they could worship Yahweh (Exodus 7–12).

Rahab understood that when the Israelite people painted the blood of lambs on their doorposts, when they were in Egypt, and the angel of death passed over their homes, it was something about the blood that had saved their lives. She also thought something about the scarlet cord she had hung out her window in Jericho called out to God to ask for forgiveness (*Rahab, My story*, 88). Rahab wanted to know and understand all things of God.

Today, we know about the blood of the Lamb, Jesus. The Lamb of God, our Savior, who shed His blood for the forgiveness of our sins so that we could be reconciled to God!

Scriptures to Consider

"The next day he [John the Baptist] saw Jesus coming toward him, and said, '_____

_____ _____ ____ _____, who takes away the sin of the world!'" (John 1:29).

"Now the passage of the Scripture that He [an Ethiopian eunuch] was reading was this: 'Like a _____he was led to the slaughter and like a _____before its shearer is silent, so He opens not his mouth'" (Acts 8:32).

"For Christ, our_____ _____, has been sacrificed" (1 Corinthians 5:7b).

"And if you call on him as Father who judges impartially according to each one's deeds, conduct yourselves with fear throughout the time of your exile, knowing that you were _____from the futile ways inherited from your forefathers, not with perishable things such as silver or gold, but with the precious _____of Christ, like that of a _____ _____ _____ ___ _____" (1 Peter 1:17–19).

"They have washed their robes and made them white in the_____ ____ _____ _____" (Revelation 7:14b).

"For the _____in the midst of the throne will be their_____, and he will guide them to springs of living water, and God will wipe away _____ _____from their eyes" (Revelation 7:17).

"For our sake he made him to be sin who knew no sin, so that in him we might become the_____ ____ _____" (2 Corinthians 5:21).

"He himself bore our sins in his body on the tree, that we might _____ ____ _____and live to righteousness. By his wounds you have been_____" (1 Peter 2:24).

Oh, to understand such things of God! Pray. Ask for wisdom (James 1:5). Pray often. Let's turn from our sinful lives. Rahab did. I did. Pray without ceasing (1 Thessalonians 5:17). "Trust in the LORD with all your heart, and do not lean on your own understanding. In all your ways acknowledge him, and he will make straight your paths" (Proverbs 3:5–6).

Do it today, not tomorrow! Now, not later!

I am praying with you and for you. Please pray for me too.

How did God speak to you through our Scriptures this discussion day?

_____

_____

_____

_____

"May the God of peace be with you all. Amen" (Romans 15:33).

Hope

LORD

Future

Welfare

For I know the plans I have for you, declares the Lord, plans for welfare and not for evil, to give you a future and a hope. Jer 29:11

NOW WHAT?

When we become a new creation after we are spiritually born-again, our *fruit* changes, and we begin living the life of JOY (Jesus, Others, Yourself)!

"And he said to him, 'You shall love the Lord your God with all your _____ and with all your _____and with all your _____.' This is the great and first commandment. And the second is like it: 'You shall love your _____as _____'" (Matthew 22:37–39).

After Rahab was accepted into the family of the Israelite people, she said, "Being part of God's family does not mean that I will never again have trials or turmoil in my life. We all suffer through difficult situations at times, but being part of God's family means that my problems will be shared by others. We are one loving family caring for each other. Wise men give counsel from the Lord and peaceful resolutions usually follow" (*Rahab, My Story*, 86). Rahab made a choice to leave all other gods behind and to obey only Yahweh—a choice we all must make.

So, my friend, this discussion guide is about how I imagined Rahab's life and her journey from sinfulness to faithfulness. Her life parallels many of our lives—at least those of us who were unaware of our great Lord and Savior, Jesus, until we were a bit older.

I really felt that I could speak about Rahab's life because we had several things in common. Rahab was probably a young lady, maybe a teenager or a bit older, when she called out to Yahweh. I was in my twenties. Rahab lived far from God, as did I. Rahab loved her material possessions. I loved mine. Rahab asked God, through the two Israelite spies she hid, to save her life. One day, after realizing that I was a sinner who needed a Savior, I called out to God to save me. God forgave Rahab, and He forgave me. God told both of us that He would never leave us or forsake us. He has made promises to those of us who love, trust, and obey Him, and He keeps every single one of them. God is so faithful!

As I grew in my faith, I began to better understand the things of God. I desired to grow and become more like Christ.

"Therefore be imitators of God, as beloved children" (Ephesians 5:1).

So much is amazing about Rahab's life. Here is one of those many amazing things.

> **The book of the genealogy of Jesus Christ,** the son of David, the son of Abraham. Abraham was the father of Isaac, and Isaac the father of Jacob, and Jacob the father of Judah and his brothers, and Judah the father of Perez and Zerah by Tamar, and Perez the father of Hezron, and Hezron the father of Ram, and Ram the father of Amminadab, and Amminadab the father of Nahshon, and Nahshon the father of Salmon, **and Salmon the father of Boaz by *Rahab*,** and Boaz the father of Obed by Ruth, and Obed the father of Jesse, and Jesse the father of David the king. And David was the father of Solomon by the wife of Uriah, and Solomon the father of Rehoboam, and Rehoboam the father of Abijah, and Abijah the father of Asaph, and Asaph the father of Jehoshaphat, and Jehoshaphat the father of Joram, and Joram the father of Uzziah, and Uzziah the father of Jotham, and Jotham the father of Ahaz, and Ahaz the father of Hezekiah, and Hezekiah the father of Manasseh, and Manasseh the father of Amos, and Amos the father of Josiah, and Josiah the father of Jechoniah and his brothers, at the time of the deportation to Babylon. And after the deportation to Babylon: Jechoniah was the father of Shealtiel, and Shealtiel the father of Zerubbabel, and Zerubbabel the father of Abiud, and Abiud the father of Eliakim, and Eliakim the father of Azor, and Azor the father of Zadok, and Zadok the father of Achim, and Achim the father of Eliud, and Eliud the father of Eleazar, and Eleazar the father of Matthan, and Matthan the father of Jacob, and Jacob the father of Joseph the husband of Mary, of whom *Jesus was born, who is called Christ*. (Matthew 1:1–17, emphasis added)

Our Lord and Savior, Jesus, came into this world through the genealogy in which Rahab, the prostitute, was included. God does whatever He pleases to work out His perfect plan for mankind.

"But God chose what is foolish in the world to shame the wise; God chose what is weak in the world to shame the strong; God chose what is low and despised in the world, even things that are not, to bring to nothing things that are, so that no human being might boast in the presence of God" (1 Corinthians 1:27–29).

In the book of Hebrews in the New Testament, where great men and women of faith are listed, Rahab, our sister in Christ Jesus, is mentioned. "By faith the prostitute Rahab, because she welcomed the spies, was not killed with those who were disobedient" (Hebrews 11:31).

God saw fit to mention the great faith of Rahab in the New Testament in the Bible. Do you find that amazing? I am astounded to read that God not only forgave Rahab, but He also commended her great faith.

Like myself, I believe Rahab was so very thankful to God for forgiving her that she wanted to do everything to please the Lord from that time on.

Our last Scriptures to Consider (I will miss our times together going through Scriptures).

"_____ I leave with you; my peace I _____ to you. Not as the world gives do I give to you. Let not your hearts be _____, neither let them be _____" (John 14:27).

"Put on then, as God's chosen ones, holy and beloved, compassionate _____, _____, _____, _____, and _____, bearing with one another and, if one has a complaint against another, _____ each other; as the Lord has _____ you, so you also must forgive. And above all these put on _____, which binds _____ together in perfect harmony" (Colossians 3:12–14).

"Let no _____talk come out of your mouths, but only such as is good for _____ _____, as fits the occasion, that it may give _____ to those who hear" (Ephesians 4:29).

"See that no one repays anyone _____ for evil, but always seek to do _____ to one another and to everyone. Rejoice _____, pray without _____, give thanks in _____circumstances; for this is the will of _____ in Christ Jesus for you" (1 Thessalonians 5:15–18).

"And without _____ it is impossible to please Him, for whoever would draw near to _____ must believe that He _____ and that he rewards those who _____ Him" (Hebrews 11:6).

"Do not be _____ to this world, but be _____ by the renewal of your mind, that by testing you may _____ what is the will of God, what is good and acceptable and perfect" (Romans 12:2).

"Finally, brothers, whatever is _____, whatever is _____, whatever is _____, whatever is _____, whatever is _____, whatever is _____, if there is any _____, if there is anything worthy of _____, think about these things" (Philippians 4:8).

Let us finish out our lives strong for our Lord, my friends. May we be able to say the following as we head for our promised land:

"I have fought the good fight, I have finished the race, I have kept the faith" (2 Timothy 4:7).

"For the grace of God has appeared, bringing salvation for all people, training us to renounce ungodliness and worldly passions, and to live self-controlled, upright, and godly lives in the present age, waiting for our blessed hope, the appearing of the glory of our great God and Savior Jesus Christ, who gave himself for us to redeem us from all lawlessness and to purify for himself a people for his own possession who are zealous for good works" (Titus 2:11–14).

"But grow in the grace and knowledge of our Lord and Savior Jesus Christ. To him be the glory both now and to the day of eternity" (2 Peter 3:18).

"And you will be my witnesses … to the end of the earth" (Acts 1:8b).

Praise God!

I hope this discussion guide has given you an unquenchable thirst for more knowledge of the Scriptures and a burning desire to increase your trust and love for our Lord Jesus.

How did God speak to you through this discussion guide?

_____

_____

_____

_____

_____

_____

_____

_____

_____

_____

_____

_____

_____

_____

_____

_____

_____

_____

_____

_____

_____

_____

_____

_____

"And behold, I am coming soon" (Revelation 22:7a).

A NOTE FROM THE AUTHOR

Dear friends,

As I said when I concluded my book, *Rahab, My Story*, I again say this to you:

Thank you for spending your time listening to my heart. You know, we need each other. God puts people in our paths for many different reasons. You have been an encouragement to me, and in fact have lifted my spirits, for not all people open their hearts and minds to listen to stories of our Lord. Maybe you sat reading this by a candle—as if you and I were by the campfires at night, listening to stories being passed down to the younger generation by the older men.

Do you have a plan for your life—an eternal plan? We've discovered that the Lord is just and that He desires our obedience and our praise. I shared with you earlier how I desired to turn from my wicked ways and follow the Lord. I didn't know how to go about that or what it would look like, so I just talked to the Lord in prayer, telling Him I needed Him. I told God that I couldn't change on my own and that I needed Him to be my guide and never leave my side. I don't remember the words I spoke; I only remember that they were simple words from a simple woman whose heart was ready to embrace the only true God.

If you haven't prayed to ask Jesus to be your Lord and Savior, maybe this is the season of your life to do so. Trust in Jesus as the One crucified, risen from the dead, and coming again as Lord of Lords and King of Kings. I will be praying, without ceasing, for you.

If you are a believer in the Lord of Lords and King of Kings already, I invite you to pray with me, without ceasing, for our friends who may be making the eternal decision to join the family of God.

May the God of hope fill you with all joy and peace as you trust in Him, so that you may overflow with hope by the power of the Holy Spirit (Romans 15:13).

Your sister in Christ,
Sandy

BIBLIOGRAPHY

Barnes, Albert. *Barnes' Notes on the Bible* (1798–1870) (public domain).

Easton, M. G., MA, DD. *Easton's Illustrated Bible Dictionary*, 1897 (public domain).

Lombardo, Sandy Saia. *Rahab, My Story: The Covenant, Two Spies, Jericho, and Salvation.* WestBow Press Publishing, 2015.

Maisel, John. *Is Jesus God? Answering the Most Important Question of Our Day.* East-West Ministries International, 2002 (with permission).

Pink, Arthur W. *The Attributes of God.* Baker Books, 1975 (public domain).

The Holy Bible, English Standard Version. Crossway Bibles, a publishing ministry of Good News Publishers, 2001.

Printed in the United States
By Bookmasters